Writing Adventures Workbook & Journal

Book 2

By Donna Cargill-Austin
&
Patricia Padgett

CREATE!
PRESS

Illustrations by Stephen Austin

Copyright ©2001 Create! Press, Inc. and its licensors. All rights reserved.
P.O. Box 2785, Carlsbad, CA 92018-2785

Clipart from Corel Mega Gallery™ Copyright ©1998 Corel Corporation and Corel Corporation Limited. All rights reserved.

The purchase of this book entitles teachers to make copies for use in their individual classrooms only. No part of this book may be reproduced for use in an entire school or school district or for commercial resale.

ISBN 0-9707097-1-4

Printed in the United States of America

TABLE OF CONTENTS

LESSON 1: **How Phrases** 1
LESSON 2: **Similes** 8
LESSON 3: **Why Phrases** 15
LESSON 4: **Subject Describer Phrases & Words** 22
LESSON 5: **Interjections** 29
LESSON 6: **Parenthetical Expressions** 34
LESSON 7: **Appositives** 39
LESSON 8: **Combining Sentences** 46
Cumulative Review Lessons 1-8
LESSON 9: **Informative Paragraph** 55
LESSON 10: **Audience** 64
LESSON 11: **Informative Essay** 71
LESSON 12: **Sequencing** 82
Cumulative Review Lessons 9-12
LESSON 13: **Operational Paragraph** 93
LESSON 14: **Operational Essay** 99
LESSON 15: **Voice & Point of View** 107
LESSON 16: **Persuasive Paragraph** 112
LESSON 17: **Persuasive Essay** 118
Cumulative Review Lessons 13-17
LESSON 18: **Stylistic Openers** 128
LESSON 19: **Compare/Contrast Paragraphs** 133
LESSON 20: **Sensory, Memory, & Reflective Details** 146
LESSON 21: **Compare/Contrast Essays** 154
LESSON 22: **Run-on Sentences** 174
LESSON 23: **Writing a Formal Letter** 181
Cumulative Review Lessons 18-23
Review Exercises 190
Answer Key 223
Paragraph & Essay Topics 231
Paragraph & Essay Templates 236
Reference Pages 260

TO EDUCATORS & PARENTS

Writing Adventures: Workbook & Journal Book 2 was developed along with Book 1 to provide a systematic, sequential, and explicit method of teaching writing skills. Book 1 systematically teaches, practices, and reviews writing concepts. It sequentially teaches writing beginning with basic, simple sentences and progressing to complex sentences, paragraphs, and story writing. Book 2 continues to teach writing skills from complex sentences to expository writing, including informative, operational, persuasive, and compare/contrast paragraphs and essays. The student's opportunity for learning and mastery is maximized because each new lesson builds upon the previously introduced and reviewed lessons. Thus, it is best if students follow the sequence of the Workbook.

In order to set up students for success, we could not assume prior knowledge or the ability to just "get it". Thus each step is explicitly taught. Furthermore, this is not a tool for students to work independently. It is imperative that the educator be actively involved to ensure that the introduced concepts are understood before the student begins the lesson activities.

The concepts in this Workbook are nothing new. We simply took the rudiments of sentence, paragraph, and essay structure and developed this systematic workbook in order for students to understand how language works when writing a complete thought. Students learn the concepts that build complete thoughts and sentences by calling phrases and parts of speech by what they do, not by the technical language. The technical language will come later, after the concepts have been learned and mastered.

Students often experience difficulty with transferring new concepts to other activities. Again, we could not assume the ability to transfer these writing concepts and skills from the workbook activities to assignments. Therefore we incorporated journaling to build the bridge from practice to application. Because students are now guided into the journaling process, they will experience success when expressing personal thoughts in the forms of sentences, paragraphs, and essays. Also, the workbook offers numerous paragraph and essay topics to further extend the application of the writing concepts and skills.

Is this Workbook only a remedial tool? Not at all. It is an excellent source for reviewing writing skills with older students and introducing writing skills with elementary and middle school students.

The Workbook operates in four ways to stimulate the learning and mastery of writing concepts and skills:

1. **The Lesson:**

   The Lesson, in a brief, concise manner, teaches a new sentence, paragraph, or story element. It then provides examples to illustrate the use of the element.

2. **Activities:**

   The Activities provide a variety of tasks for practicing and mastering the lesson.

3. **Discovery:**

   Discovery is a valuable learning tool. The discovery process asks the student questions that lead to the discovery and verification of additional information about the new element. Following each discovery, the student completes an activity which focuses on that discovery.

4. **Journal Entry:**

   The Journal Entry often asks the learner to answer questions or provide personal information while using all they have learned about sentence and paragraph structure up to that point in the book.

Icons

Lesson: Put your thinking cap on! It's time to learn something new.

Activity: Get your pencil ready. It's time to practice what you've learned.

Discovery: Pay close attention! You're about to discover some very important information.

Journal: Usually this is a sign for turning inward and writing some personal thoughts.

HOW PHRASES

 **Lesson**

In Workbook One you learned about when and where phrases.
These phrases are called prepositional phrases.
Another prepositional phrase can tell **how** the action occurred.
We will call these **how phrases**.

How Phrase: A string of words that tells how the action occurred.

Think about what you learned in Workbook One about adverbs.
An **adverb** is a *single word* that tells how the action occurred.
A **how phrase** is a *string of words* that tells how the action occurred.

EXAMPLE: *The clock ticks continuously.*

Continuously is an **adverb** that tells how the clock ticked.

The clock ticks without stopping.

Without stopping is a **prepositional phrase** that tells how the clock ticks.

How phrases often begin with the following prepositions.

with   without   in

EXAMPLE: *The earth shook without warning.*

The earth shook with force.

The earth shook in a rolling motion.

To sum up the lesson, you now have two ways to write how the action occurred.
—First, you can use an **adverb** ending in -ly.
—Second, you can use a **how phrase**.

Activity One

Circle the word or words that tell how the action occurred. Then write whether it is an **adverb** or a **prepositional** phrase.

EXAMPLE: *The quarterback (quickly) threw the ball.* —Adverb

1. The autumn leaves glistened in full color.

2. The students diligently studied.

3. The little boy blinked nervously.

4. A snake sniffs with its tongue.

5. Jane crossed the quiet street without caution.

6. The snow storm struck suddenly.

7. Without a care in the world, Lisa napped in her hammock.

8. With tears in her eyes, Rachel confessed that she

   teased her brother.

9. In a crashing boom, the thunder exploded.

10. Quickly, he shut the book and turned out the light.

11. Rick finished his homework with haste.

12. The two candidates nervously shook hands.

13. Instantly, the phantom vanished.

Discovery

Look back at sentences 1, 3, and 4. Where did the **adverb** or **how phrase** appear in the sentence? _____

Now look at sentences 7, 8, and 9. Where did the the **adverb** or **how phrase** appear in the sentence? _____

Write a complete sentence that states where an **adverb** or **how phrase** can appear in a sentence.

_____
_____

Activity Two

Diagram the following sentences using the diagram key at the right. Above each phrase write whether it is a **when, where,** or **how** phrase.

EXAMPLE: The <u>silly</u> clown juggled <u>three</u> balls carelessly
               S   V   O   AV

    where
[in the air].

DIAGRAM KEY	
S	Subject
V	Verb
O	Object
_	Adjective
C	Completer
AV	Adverb
[ ]	Phrase

1. We will have a spelling test on Friday.

2. Tomorrow, we will visit the zoo.

3. The orchestra played in harmony.

4. Dad put the car keys in his pocket.

5. With hope for the future, President Lincoln signed the Emancipation Proclamation.

6. Martin Luther King Jr. worked diligently and peacefully.

7. George Washington crossed the Delaware River without fear.

8. I am going to Paris on Thursday.

9. The lion tamer courageously placed his head inside the lion's mouth.

10. The old fisherman fishes in the morning.

11. With heavy eye lids, the little girl kissed her parents goodnight.

12. The gazelle gracefully ran across the savanna.

13. Anne Frank wrote in her diary with dedication.

14. Triumphantly, Helen Keller learned reading, writing, and arithmetic.

15. The clock chimed melodically.

Writing Adventures Book 2

Activity Three

Next to each picture write a sentence with a **how phrase**. Use the preposition below the picture.

without

with

with

in

with

_____

without

_____

in

_____

with

_____

 **Journal Entry**

Complete the following sentences about yourself using **how phrases**.

I study with _____

I eat without _____

I sing in _____

I sleep with _____

I hit a ball with _____

I go to school without _____

I dance to _____

I like to paint with _____

I run in _____

I clean my room with _____

I like to read with _____

LESSON 2
SIMILES

 **Lesson**

You now know of two ways to tell how the action occurred. You can use an **-ly adverb** or you can use a **how phrase**. There is one more way to tell how the action occurred. You can compare the subject with another noun by using the words *like* and *as*.

EXAMPLE: *The athlete ran like a shooting star.*

This sentence compares the running of the athlete to the way a star shoots through the sky.

This technique is called a **simile**.

Simile: a phrase that tells how the action occurred by using the words "like" or "as" to compare the subject with the qualities of another noun.

 Activity One

Circle the word or words that tell how the action occurred. Then write whether it is an **adverb**, a **prepositional phrase**, or a **simile**.

EXAMPLE: *The baby cried (like a howling wolf.)*—Simile

1. Some people say that frog legs taste like chicken.

2. Like booming thunder, the audience clapped.

3. The oak tree swayed wildly in the wind.

4. The heavy rain fell like a gushing waterfall.

5. The stray dog walked with a limp.

6. The eagle soared with grace.

Writing Adventures Book 2

7. The glass fell without breaking.

8. The helicopter hovered above the building like a bee above a flower.

9. My dog jumped like a grasshopper.

10. The children listened with eagerness.

11. My voice sounded like a frog croaking.

12. Like a pro, he hit the hockey puck into the goal.

13. With great care, John folded his clothes.

14. He told his joke without laughing.

15. One day, cars will fly like airplanes.

Discovery

Look back at sentences 1, 4, and 8. Where did the **simile** appear in each sentence? _____

Now look at sentences 2 and 12. Where did the **simile** appear in each sentence? _____

Write a complete sentence that states where a **simile** can appear in a sentence.

_____

_____

Discovery Two

Look back at sentences 2 and 12. What punctuation do you see after the **simile**? _____

Write a complete sentence that states the punctuation that follows a **simile** when it is at the beginning of a sentence.

_____

_____

Activity Two

Complete each sentence using a **simile**.

1. The man yelled like _____

2. The running dinosaurs sounded like _____

3. The summer heat felt like _____

4. Like_____, the skier glided down the hill.

5. He swims like _____

6. The lights twinkled like_____

7. Like_____, Jason hit the ball.

8. The ship sank as fast as _____

9. The car sounded like_____

10. Like_____, the fire spread through the forest.

11. The toddlers ran like _____

12. The sidewalk is as hot as_____

13. Like_____, we huddled under the blanket during the scary movie.

14. The asteroid is as big as_____

15. The waves crashed like_____

Writing Adventures Book 2

Activity Three

Diagram the following sentences using the diagram key at the right. Above each phrase write whether it is a **when, where,** or **how** phrase or a **simile**.

EXAMPLE: The fox ran swiftly [through the woods]
             S   V   AV   where
          when
[as the hunter lost sight of him].

DIAGRAM KEY
- S Subject
- V Verb
- O Object
- _ Adjective
- C Completer
- AV Adverb
- [ ] Phrase/Simile

1. The snow fell heavily on Christmas Eve night.

2. The bear growled ferociously while protecting her young.

3. My mom goes to bed early every night.

4. During rush hour, the cars move like turtles.

5. The lightning flashed suddenly in the distance.

6. In the corners of the basement, the spiders spin their webs.

7. During the Civil War, Harriet Tubman saved many lives with the Underground Railroad.

8. My ring fell between the rocks during our hike.

9. On Valentine's Day, Emily signed the letter with love.

10. Without warning, the cold winter descended upon us.

11. Against her mother's advice, she rode her bike without a helmet.

12. During the ninth inning, the team pulled together and won the game.

13. During the afternoon, the black street is as hot as a frying pan.

14. After the game, the large crowd moved quickly like a stampede.

15. Like a kaleidescope, our large garden is filled with beautiful, bright flowers.

Activity Four

Listed below are 10 **similes**. Use each **simile** in a sentence. In order to create each sentence think of a person, place, or thing that might have similar qualities as the **simile**. For example, "like a bird" can make you think of an airplane, a kite, or a child playing.

EXAMPLE: *like a bird*

       Like a bird, my kite soared through the air.

1. bright like lightning

_____

_____

2. pale as a ghost

_____

_____

3. shook like an earthquake

_____

_____

4. green as grass

_____

_____

5. beat like a drum

_____

_____

6. quiet as a mouse

_____

_____

7. sounded like fingernails on a blackboard

_____

_____

8. like finding a needle in a hay stack

_____

_____

9. as fast as a race horse

_____

_____

10. like a cloud

_____

_____

 # Journal Entry

Complete each sentence by using a **simile** to describe yourself. Imagine yourself in each situation and think of a person, place, or thing that has the same qualities.

I eat like _____

_____

I sleep like _____

_____

My friends and I play like _____

_____

I run like _____

_____

I play baseball like _____

_____

I can juggle like _____

_____

I sing like _____

_____

I am growing like _____

_____

I paint like _____

_____

I read as _____

_____

LESSON 3
WHY PHRASES

 **Lesson**

So far you have learned about three types of prepositional phrases — **when, where,** and **how** phrases.
Another type of prepositional phrase is a **why** phrase.
Why phrases tell why the action occurred.
Some words that often begin **why** phrases are:

    so
    for
    to
    because

EXAMPLE: *The boy turned off the radio so he could study.*
              Why did the boy turn off the radio?
              So he could study.

Why Phrase: a phrase that tells why the action occurred.

 **Activity One**

Circle the word or words that tell why the action occurred.

EXAMPLE: Mom baked a cake (for Dad's birthday.)

1. The children ran through the sprinklers because they were hot.

2. The snake rests under the bush to cool its body.

3. Mom cut up the hot dog for the baby.

4. The class boarded the bus for the field trip.

5. Dad went to the sale so he could save money.

6. The polar bear dove in the water to get the fish.

7. Because he was too small, my little brother could not go on the roller coaster.

8. Elizabeth Cady Stanton worked hard for women's rights.

9. Eleanor Roosevelt created programs to help the poor.

10. To preserve our natural resources, Theodore Roosevelt created the National Parks system.

11. Mom went to the store to get some milk.

12. Jake tied his shoes so he wouldn't trip and fall.

13. We visit the wildlife refuge to learn about endangered species.

14. Because he was tired and hungry, the baby cried loudly.

15. She asked me for help.

Discovery

Look back at sentences 1, 2, and 3. Where did the **why** phrase appear in the sentence? _____

Now look at sentences 7, 10, and 14. Where did the **why** phrase appear in the sentence? _____

Write a complete sentence that states where a **why** phrase can appear in a sentence.

_____

_____

Activity Two

Diagram the following sentences using the diagram key at the right. Above each phrase, write whether it is a **when, where, how,** or **why** phrase or a **simile**.

EXAMPLE: [During the night,] the tree branch scratched the window pane [like fingernails on a chalkboard].
(when) S V O simile

1. The cat sat on the floor to clean her paws.

2. In Antarctica, penguins fish in cold waters.

3. Like humans, chimpanzees are primates.

4. Dolphins use echolocation to communicate and find their way.

5. The Bill of Rights was written to insure our individual freedoms.

6. Gallileo studied constellations so he could better understand the universe.

7. In 1492, Christopher Columbus set sail to discover a new route to Asia.

8. During the 16th century, Queen Elizabeth I was a very powerful leader.

DIAGRAM KEY

- S Subject
- V Verb
- O Object
- _ Adjective
- C Completer
- AV Adverb
- [ ] Phrase/Simile

9. In China, pandas are protected because they are endangered species.

10. Coral reefs can be found in warm, shallow waters.

11. A chameleon changes color to protect itself from predators.

12. My mother planted tulip bulbs before spring.

13. Because it was over hunted, the American Buffalo nearly became extinct.

14. We use our lungs to breathe.

15. Daniel Boone was a famous frontiersman.

 Activity Three

Next to each picture, write a sentence with a **why phrase.** Use the preposition provided beneath the picture.

for _____

because _____

to _____

so _____

to _____

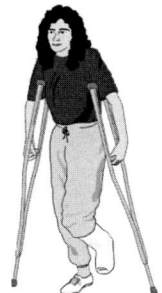
because _____

for _____

to _____

Journal Entry

Use **why phrases** to complete the following sentences about yourself.

I like to go to the store to

I took swimming lessons so

I ride my bike because

I save my money so

I write letters to

I eat vegetables because

I clean my room so

I study to

I read because

I call my friend for

I go to school because

LESSON 4
SUBJECT DESCRIBER PHRASES AND WORDS

 **Lesson**

In Workbook One you learned to use adjectives to describe the subject. You can also use a prepositional phrase to describe the subject. These **subject describer phrases** set the subject apart by telling exactly which subject the sentence is about.

EXAMPLE: *The dog barked loudly.*

This sentence doesn't tell you which dog barked.

Maybe it was a stray dog or the neighbor's dog.

The dog with the big teeth barked loudly.
Which dog barked?
Answer: The one with the big teeth.
With the big teeth is the **subject describer phrase**.

Sometimes a **subject describer** can be a single word that indicates which subject the sentence is about.

EXAMPLE: *That* dog barks loudly.

These pants don't fit.

This apple is sour.

That, these, this, and *those* are subject describer words.

Subject Describer Phrase or Word:
A phrase or word that tells which subject the sentence is about.

Activity One

Circle the **subject describer phrase** or word in each sentence. Underline the **adjectives** that also describe the subject.

EXAMPLE: The <u>large</u> pelican (with the fish in its mouth) sat on the pier.

1. The sand dunes in Morro Bay move a few inches each year.

2. The little girl with the green hat is a girl scout.

3. The rings of Saturn are made up of ice, rock, and dust.

4. The cable cars of San Francisco are a familiar sight.

5. The girl on the horse is wearing a helmet.

6. People in Japan eat a lot of fish and rice.

7. The signers of the Declaration of Independence were notable men.

8. The President of the United States is a powerful person.

9. That mouse stole the cheese.

10. Those windmills generate electricity.

11. The racoon with the large tail rummaged through the trash.

12. These books are for the children.

13. The sign on the door is a warning.

 **Discovery**

Look back at the sentences that contain **subject describer** *phrases*. Where did the **subject describer phrase** appear in the sentence?

_____

Now look at the sentences containing **subject describer** *words*. Where did the **subject describer words** appear in the sentence?

_____

Write a complete sentence that states where we place a **subject describer phrase** or **word** in a sentence.

_____

_____

 Activity Two

Diagram the following sentences using the diagram key at the right. Above each phrase, write whether it is a **when, where, how,** or **why** phrase or a **simile**. Put a box around the **subject describer phrase** or **word**.

                     S   V   O

EXAMPLE: The man |in the tuxedo| drove the limousine

                  where
         [to the party].

1. The shells along the shore are broken.

2. We get milk from cows.

3. In legends, mermaids were a sign of disaster.

4. The cat on the fence is hunting mice.

5. A new born kangaroo stays in its mother's pouch.

DIAGRAM KEY	
S	Subject
V	Verb
O	Object
_	Adjective
C	Completer
AV	Adverb
[ ]	Phrase/Simile
☐	Subject Describer

6. Pheidippides was the man who ran with the news of Greek victory after the Battle of Marathon.

7. Los Angeles is the second largest city in the United States.

8. Female lions do most of the hunting.

9. Charles Lindbergh made a historic flight across the Atlantic Ocean.

10. The Statue of Liberty was a gift from France.

11. The Mona Lisa hangs in the Louvre Museum in Paris.

12. In autumn, deciduous trees lose their leaves.

13. My brother's room looked like a bomb hit it.

14. President John F. Kennedy was born in Brookline, Massachusetts.

15. The Mayan people of Central America grew corn and sweet potatoes on communal lands.

 # Activity Three

Next to each picture, write a sentence with a **subject describer phrase** or **word**.

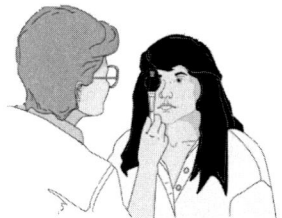

_____

_____

_____

_____

_____

_____

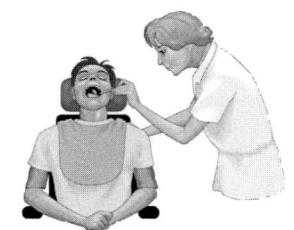
_____

_____

Journal Entry

Listed below are 7 items you might find in your home or neighborhood. Put each noun in a complete sentence with a **subject describer phrase** or **word**.

park

bike

cat

car

tree

clock

book

LESSON 5
INTERJECTIONS

 **Lesson**

When we want to express a strong emotion in a sentence we can use a word called an **interjection.**

EXAMPLE: *Wow! That roller coaster was awesome.*

Wow! interrupts the sentence to express excitement. The word interject means to interrupt.

Some **interjections** interrupt the sentence to show agreement or disagreement.

EXAMPLE: *No, I don't think we should go.*

Yes, red is my favorite color.

Interjection: a word that interrupts a sentence to express a strong emotion or to indicate agreement or disagreement.

 **Activity One**

Put a check (✓) over the **interjection** in each sentence.

          ✓

EXAMPLE: *Yikes! I better get home.*

1. Ouch! That hurt.

2. No, I don't have a dog.

3. Oh! That's my favorite flower.

4. Hey! Where were you last night?

5. Wow! Your new haircut looks great.

6. Yes, we will be leaving soon.

7. Phew! That was hard.

8. Goodness! You are a handful.

9. Well, should we go?

10. Gee whiz! It was just an accident.

Discovery I

Look back at all the **interjections** followed by an exclamation point. Did these words express strong emotion? _____
Now look at the sentences with a comma following the **interjection**. Did these words express strong emotion? _____

Write a complete sentence that states what you have just learned about punctuation after an **interjection**.

_____
_____

Discovery II

Now look at the word following each **interjection** that had an exclamation point. What do you notice about the first letter?

_____

Now look at the word that followed each **interjection** that had a comma. What do you notice about the first letter?

_____

Writing Adventures Book 2

Write a complete sentence that states what you have just learned about capitalization after an **interjection.**

_____
_____

Summary of Discovery I & II

An **interjection** that expresses strong emotion is followed by an exclamation point.
An **interjection** that does not express strong emotion is followed by a comma.
Capitalize the first word that follows an **interjection** that expresses strong emotion.
Do not capitalize the first word that follows an **interjection** that does not express strong emotion.

Discovery III

Write all the **interjections** you checked in Activity One.

_____
_____
_____
_____

Here are more **interjections:**

hurry	aha	oops
ah	help	alas
eek	eureka	alright
oh, no		

Activity Two

Take 10 **interjections** from the Discoveries or make up a few of your own and use them to write 10 sentences. Remember the punctuation and capitalization rules you learned in the Discoveries.

Journal Entry

Answer each question or respond to the statement using an **interjection**. Use the Discovery section if you need help with capitalization and punctuation.

Are your eyes blue?

_____

_____

School starts in 5 minutes and you are not dressed.

_____

_____

You are having pizza for dinner.

_____

_____

You just finished a big project.

_____

_____

The ice cream truck is coming.

_____

_____

You see a rainbow on the horizon.

_____

_____

You just rode a roller coaster.

_____

_____

LESSON 6
PARENTHETICAL EXPRESSIONS

 **Lesson**

Some words or phrases are added to sentences to give more explanation.

EXAMPLE: Some people say that the color of your car reflects your personality. **For example,** I have a red car and a fiery personality.

For example lets the reader know that the following statement is an example of the statement before it. In this case, the writer's red car reflects his fiery personality.

In my opinion, this movie is boring.

In my opionion lets the reader know that the following statement is only an opinion and not a fact.

These phrases are called **parenthetical expressions.** **Parenthetical expressions** are always set off by commas, because they are not necessary in order to have a complete sentence.

EXAMPLE: We, too, went to the carnival.

Parenthetical Expression: a word or phrase that adds a little more explanation to the words that follow.

 **Activity One**

Circle the **parenthetical expressions** in each of the following sentences.

EXAMPLE: (If it were up to me,) I would choose the red one.

1. In my opinion, bats are fascinating creatures.

2. John, therefore, decided to do the project.

3. To tell the truth, I'd rather see the other movie.

4. James, however, is not a good friend.

5. In fact, several people agree with the candidate.

6. For example, we could spend the day at the beach.

7. I suppose, the teacher can help you with your work.

8. In the first place, Chris doesn't have a bike.

9. She, too, received an A on the test.

10. If you ask me, he will make a good class president.

Activity Two

Write sentences using the following **parenthetical expressions.**

1. Therefore

2. I suppose

3. If you ask me

4. Too

5. If it were up to me

6. In fact

7. To tell the truth

8. In the first place

9. For example

Activity Three

Diagram the following sentences using the diagram key at the right.

1. If you ask me, that dog is not friendly.

2. The deer hiding in the forest were still until the hunters left.

3. During the storm, we played games and ate popcorn.

4. I found the green bike in the river.

5. Yikes! That water is cold.

6. I placed the hot apple pie on the table.

7. Those dolphins enjoy riding the waves on the beaches of Florida.

8. The captain of the ship ordered the crew to man the battle stations.

9. The young writer nervousuly accepted the Pulizter Prize.

10. Sophia, too, enjoys horseback riding on the trail.

11. Sean, however, went in without a wet suit.

12. To tell the truth, I like the red one best.

DIAGRAM KEY

S	Subject
V	Verb
O	Object
—	Adjective
C	Completer
AV	Adverb
[ ]	Phrase/Simile
☐	Subject Describer
✓	Interjection
◯	Parenthetical Expression

Journal Entry

Use **parenthetical expressions** to comment on the following topics. Refer to Activity Two for a list of parenthetical expressions.

school uniforms

_____

_____

the environment

_____

_____

homework

_____

_____

team sports

_____

_____

television

_____

_____

pop music

_____

_____

the last book you read

_____

_____

LESSON 7
APPOSITIVES

 **Lesson**

Sometimes in a sentence we may want to refer to a subject or object in more than one way in order to provide more information. Perhaps we may first refer to it as a **common noun** and then as a **proper noun**.

EXAMPLE: *My dog Spot is very rambunctious.*

Dog is the **common noun** and *Spot* is its proper name. Or perhaps we may first use a **common noun** and then a phrase.

EXAMPLE: *Our car, a rusty old station wagon, is in the shop.*

Car is a **common noun** and *rusty old station wagon* is a phrase that restates the subject in a different way to provide more information about the car.

Repeating a subject or object using different words is called an **appositive**.

Appositive: A word or words that repeat the subject or object in a different way.

 **Activity One**

Circle the **appositive** and underline the noun (subject or object) that is being repeated in each of the following sentences.

EXAMPLE: Mt. Saint Helens, (an active volcano) erupted in 1980.

1. Kabuki, a form of theatre, is very popular in Japan.

2. In the musical *Oklahoma,* Curly and Judd are rivals.

3. Machu Pichu, an ancient ruin in Peru, is visited by many tourists.

4. My friend Elizabeth has that book.

5. Frances, my younger sister, is taller than I.

6. Beacon Street, one of the longest streets in Boston, is lined with trees.

7. Our clock, an antique grandfather clock, chimes on the hour.

8. Yesterday, I met Mrs. Green, the new fourth grade teacher.

9. Today, our class read from *Bridge to Terebithia*, my favorite book.

10. The Statue of Liberty, a famous American landmark, greets immigrants from all over the world.

11. The Netherlands, a country in Europe, is famous for tulips and windmills.

12. The musical *Cats* was the longest running musical on Broadway.

13. We visited the Egyptian Pyramids, one of the Seven Wonders of the world.

Discovery

Look back at sentences 1, 3 and 5. What punctuation came before and after the appositive? Was the **appositive** necessary to know the exact subject?

_____

Now look at the sentences 2 and 12. Was there any punctuation before and after the **appositive**? Was the **appositive** necessary to know the exact name of the subject?

_____

Write a complete sentence that states when you should use commas to set off an **appositive**.

_____
_____

Summary of Discovery

When an **appositive** is not necessary to know the exact subject or object, it must be set off by commas.

EXAMPLE: *Our clock, an antique grandfather clock, chimes on the hour.*

> In this sentence we probably have only one clock that chimes. So adding that it is an antique grandfather clock is not necessary.

When an **appositive** is necessary to know the exact subject or object, it should not by set off by commas.

EXAMPLE: *My friend Elizabeth has that book.*

> In this sentence the writer probably has more than one friend so adding Elizabeth is necessary to let the reader know which friend the sentence is about.

Activity Two

Diagram the following sentences using the diagram key at the right. Above each phrase, write whether it is a **when, where, how,** or **why** phrase or a **simile**. Put a triangle above the **appositive**.

                        S   △   V   O
EXAMPLE: A Stradivarius, a type of violin, plays the best music.

1. Mice look for shelter during the winter.

2. Gee whiz! I was only kidding.

3. That dog barks like a squeaking mouse.

4. Tea grown in China is the best in the world.

5. Ivan the Terrible was the first czar of Russia.

6. In the first place, I can't find the address.

7. My brother David takes martial arts lessons after school.

DIAGRAM KEY	
S	Subject
V	Verb
O	Object
—	Adjective
C	Completer
AV	Adverb
[ ]	Phrase/Simile
☐	Subject Describer
✓	Interjection
◯	Parenthetical Expression
△	Appositive

8. Indiana's most famous annual event is the Indianapolis 500.

9. The Ganges, a river in India, is sacred to Hindus.

10. Because it is unpredictable, a hurricane can cause a lot of damage.

11. The giraffe is the tallest animal in the world.

12. Once again, the capital of Germany is now Berlin.

13. The Hindu lawyer Mohandas Gandhi helped to free India through peaceful means.

Activity Three
Next to each picture, write a sentence with an **appositive.**

_____

_____

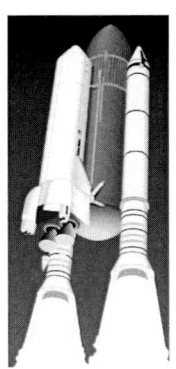

_____

_____

_____

_____

_____

_____

 # Journal Entry

Listed below are different nouns. Use each noun in a complete sentence with an **appositive.**

EXAMPLE: *brother*

    My brother Chris is a chef.

sister/brother

___

___

friend

___

___

favorite city

___

___

favorite food

___

___

favorite animal

___

___

worst nightmare

___

___

the president

___

___

LESSON 8
COMBINING SENTENCES

 **Lesson**

Short, choppy sentences can make an essay difficult to read. Combining sentences wherever possible can make your essay smoother and more enjoyable for the reader.

In Writing Adventures Book One you learned to combine two like sentences to make one compound sentence using the **conjunctions** *and, but, or.*

EXAMPLE: *Kim's shirt is yellow. Karen's shirt is blue.*

Kim's shirt is yellow, and Karen's shirt is blue.

You can also use prepositional phrases—**when, where, why,** or **how phrases**—to combine sentences that show cause and effect.

EXAMPLE: *John told a joke. Kim laughed.*

Kim laughed when John told the joke.

Another way to combine sentences is to use a **subject describer phrase**.

EXAMPLE: *Paul skillfully rode his horse. He lived on a cattle ranch.*

Paul, who lived on a cattle ranch, skillfully rode his horse.

 **Activity One**

Use a **prepositional phrase** or a **subject describer phrase** to combine each of the following sentences.

1. Dinner was cooked. We sat down at the table.

2. Juan finished his homework. He is in the fourth grade.

3. The earthquake stopped rumbling. We went outside to look for damage.

4. Serfs and lords lived on manors. They lived during medieval times.

5. The Titantic sank in the icy Atlantic Ocean. It was on its maiden voyage.

6. Jamie went to the library. She checked out a story book.

7. The Jamestown colonists settled on the James River. They were from England.

8. Mr. Martinez bought a bike. He rides to the store.

9. The school bus arrived. The children cheered.

10. My grandfather makes beautiful wooden toys. He is a carpenter.

11. The photographer saw children playing in the fountain. He quickly began taking pictures.

12. The eastern seaboard has a thriving fishing industry. It has lobster, crab, and cod.

Activity Two

The following paragraphs are choppy and difficult to read. Rewrite each paragraph, combining sentences wherever possible.

1. Jan lives on a farm. She knows a lot about taking care of animals. Jan gets up in the morning. She goes into the stable and cleans her horse's stall. She feeds the horse. She cleans its hooves. After that she feeds the chickens. She feeds them chicken pellets. Then she gathers the eggs. Jan likes to take care of the animals. The animals like Jan too.

2. The early Native American tribes were resourceful. They took from the earth. They gave back to the earth. They planted crops. They fished in rivers. They hunted deer. They hunted buffalo. Indian tribes used the meat for food. They used the hides for clothing and shelter. They sang songs and danced. They thanked mother earth for providing these resources.

3. Cruise ships offer unique vacations. Vacations are luxurious and full of adventure. Ships have many activities. You can swim. People play shuffle board. Indoor rock climbing is fun. Kids can play games. They have arts and crafts. The food is fabulous. You can have gourmet meals. Cruise ships offer seafood. They have many salads. There are desserts. They go to unique places. You can go to Mexico. They go to the Bahamas. They go to Alaska.

Journal Entry

Complete the sentences in each item. Then combine the sentences into one using a **prepositional phrase** or a **subject describer phrase**.

My favorite movie is _____

I have seen it _____

_____

_____

When I was born my eyes were _____

Now, my eyes are _____

_____

_____

Our family pet is a _____

Its name is _____

_____

_____

I was born on _____

That day the weather was _____

_____

_____

My family celebrates _____

We celebrate this occasion by _____

_____

_____

LESSONS 1-8
CUMULATIVE REVIEW

Take this cumulative review test to make sure you understand the lessons you have learned. If you miss items on the test, go back and review the lessons you had difficulty with and do the comprehensive exercises in the back of your book.

1. Circle the **how phrase** in the following sentence.

    Johnny rode his bike with caution.

2. Name three **prepositions** that commonly begin a **how phrase**.

    _____

    _____

3. What do we call a phrase that begins with the words *like* or *as* and expresses how the action occurred?

    _____

    _____

4. Circle the **why phrase** in the following sentence.

    Because she was frightened, Tina slept with the light on.

5. Name three **prepositions** that commonly begin a **why phrase**.

    _____

    _____

6. Circle the **subject describer phrase** in the following sentence.

    The shell with the ridges is the prettiest.

7. Circle the **subject describer word** in the following sentence.

   That horse has a long mane.

8. What do you call a word that interrupts a sentence to express a strong emotion or to express agreement or disagreement?

   _____

   _____

9. *In my opinion* is an example of what part of speech?

   _____

   _____

10. Circle the **appositive** in the following sentence and underline the word it is repeating.

    Diego Rivera, a Mexican artist, is well known for his murals.

11. What types of phrases can be used to combine sentences?

    _____

    _____

12. Combine the following sentences using a **subject describer phrase**.

    Go pick up the little boy. He is the one that is crying.

    _____

    _____

LESSON 9
ORGANIZING AND WRITING AN INFORMATIVE PARAGRAPH

 **Lesson**

In Workbook I you learned to write narrative paragraphs and stories. In Workbook II you will learn to write **expository** paragraphs and essays. Expository means informative, a paragraph or essay written to inform the reader.

Expository Writing: Writing that informs the reader

There are several different types of expository writing. In this book you will learn **informative, persuasive, compare/contrast,** and **operational** expository writing.

In this lesson we will focus on writing an **informative paragraph**. An **informative paragraph** provides the reader with factual details of a particular subject.

Informative Paragraph: A paragraph that provides the reader with factual details of a particular subject.

The first step is to brainstorm your ideas. What you see on the following page is a web of thoughts about softball.

Web

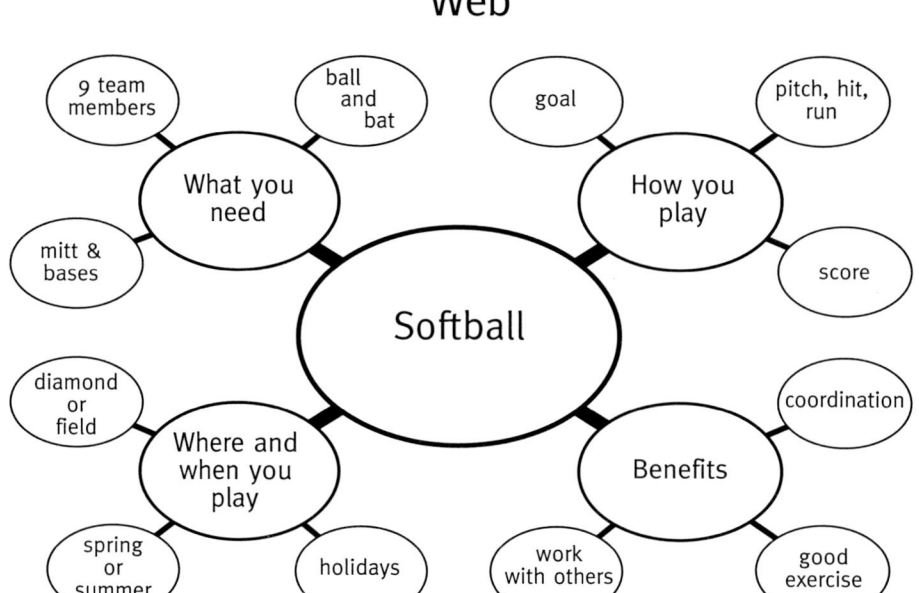

The web addresses the important questions such as **who, what, where, when, how,** and **why,** as well as any additional thoughts.
The question **why** is usually answered by explaining the rest of your thoughts. For example, you need a bat to hit the ball.

Activity One

Now it is your turn to brainstorm ideas for your informative paragraph. Your topic will be your **favorite animal.** Write the name of your animal in the center box. Then answer all the important questions: who, what, where, when, how, and why.

Web

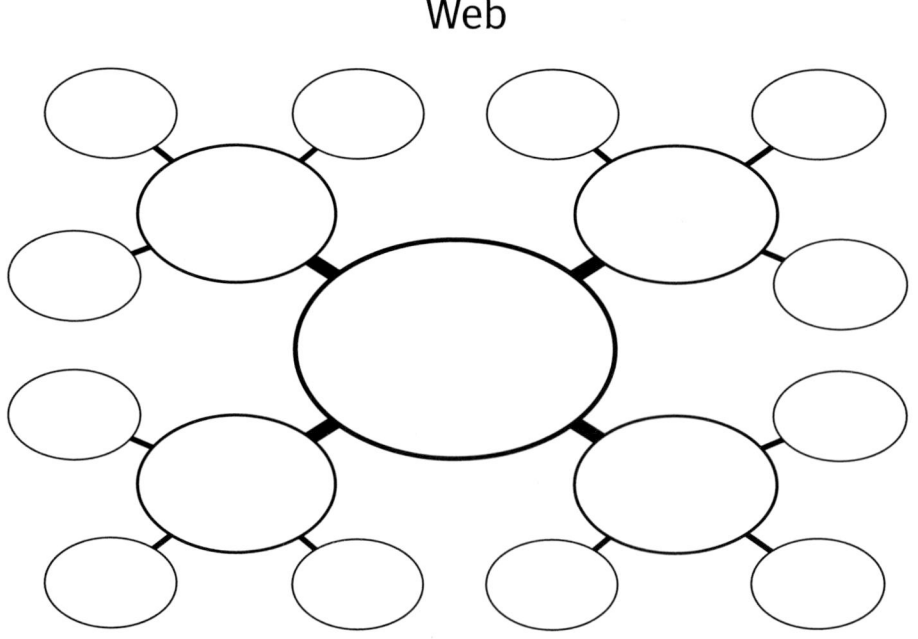

The next step is to pick a focus. Since the assignment is to write a paragraph the focus must be narrow. For example, a paragraph can focus on explaining how to play the game of softball.

Step 2: Pick a focus

Pick a focus from your web and write it here:

_____

The next step is to organize or outline your ideas. The following paragraph outline focuses on how to play the game of softball.

Step 3: Outline your ideas

Most paragraphs have a **main idea or topic sentence**, a few **details**, and a **conclusion**.

Topic Sentence/Main Idea
Softball is a fun and easy sport to play.

Detail Sentence   (first, one)
What you need.

Detail Sentence   (second, next, also)
One team takes the field.

| Detail Sentence | (third, after that, as well) |

ball is pitched, batter swings, run bases, other team tries to tag

| Detail Sentence | (last, finally) |

after three outs next team up, play 7 innings, team with most points wins

| Conclusion Sentence |

an enjoyable sport that anyone can play

The **topic sentence/main idea** told what the paragraph was going to be about. Everything else in the paragraph will have to discuss how to play the game of softball.

Topic Sentence: The sentence that tells what the paragraph will be about

Now turn your focus topic into a main idea and write it here:

The three **details** support the topic sentence by giving more information about the game of softball. It is best to have 3-5 details in your paragraph.

Details: Events or facts that support the topic sentence.

Select 3-5 details from your brainstorm and write them here:

_____
_____
_____
_____

The **conclusion** is the last sentence in the paragraph. It can also be called a clincher, because it wraps up the paragraph with a logical ending.

Conclusion/Clincher: Wrap up the paragraph with a logical ending

Write a conclusion sentence that wraps up your ideas here:

_____
_____

*Notice that when you brainstorm and outline your paragraph you do not need to use complete sentences.

Activity Two

Now it is your turn to outline a paragraph. Transfer your ideas from this lesson to the outline below.

Topic Sentence/Main Idea
_____
_____

Detail Sentence (first, one)
_____
_____

Detail Sentence (second, next, also)
_____
_____

Detail Sentence (third, after that, as well)
_____
_____

Detail Sentence (last, finally)
_____
_____

Conclusion Sentence
_____
_____

After you outline your ideas, you are ready to write the rough draft of your paragraph.

Step 4: Write a rough draft

Here are a few things to know:
    Indent the first word in a paragraph.
    Turn the main idea, each detail, and the conclusion into complete sentences.
    A rough draft may have mistakes. You will edit and revise your work later.

(*Note: The following rough draft contains errors. Can you find them?)

Softball is a fun and easy to play. In order to play you need a bat, a mitt, a ball, and 9 players for each team and also 4 bases. First, one team bats while the other team takes the field. Then the ball is pitched and the batter swings the bat trying to hit the ball. If the batter hits the ball he runs to first base. he keeps on running bases along as it is safe. When a runner makes it around all the bases, a point is scored. The other teams tries to tag him out. When the runner makes it around all the bases, a point is scored. After three outs the other team bats. The play for seven innings. The team with the most points win. It is an enjoyable sport that anyone can play.

Activity Three

Now it is your turn to write a rough draft. You should try to do your best, but remember this is a rough draft. You will edit and revise your work before writing the final draft.

_____
_____
_____
_____
_____

After writing your rough draft, you should reread your paragraph a few times looking for errors. Look for the following types of errors:
- -capitalization
- -spelling
- -run-on sentences
- -punctuation
- -subject/verb agreement
- -incomplete sentences

A run-on sentence is one with too many subjects and verbs. See Lesson 22.
An incomplete sentence is one without a subject or verb.
Look at the corrections in the following paragraph.

Step 5: Edit

 Softball is ~~X~~ fun and easy to play. In order to play you need a bat, a mitt, a ball, a~~n~~d 9 players for each team⌒and a~~ls~~o 4 bases. First, one team bats while the other team takes the field. Then the ball is pitched and the batter swings the bat trying to hit the ball. If the batter hits the ball he runs to first base.⊙e keeps on running bases ^as ~~X~~long as it is safe. When a runner makes it around all the bases, a point is scored. The other teams tries to tag him out. After three outs the other team bats. The^y play for seven innings. The team with the most points win. ~~X~~ is an enjoyable sport that anyone can play.
  softball

Once the paragraph is edited, the writer can write the final draft.

Step 6: Rewrite—Final draft

 Softball is fun and easy to play. In order to play you need a bat, a mitt, a ball, 9 players for each team, and 4 bases. First, one team bats while the other team takes the field. Then the ball is pitched and the batter swings the bat trying to hit the ball. If the batter hits the ball, he runs to first base. He continues to run bases as long as it is safe. When a runner makes it around all the bases, a point is scored. The other team tries to tag him out. After three outs the other team bats. Play continues for seven innings, and the team with the most points wins. Softball is an enjoyable sport that anyone can play.

Activity Four

Look back at your rough draft and reread it 2 or 3 times looking for errors. Try reading it aloud and noticing if it sounds right. You don't want it to sound too casual like everyday speech, but you also don't want it to sound awkward. Trust your instincts. When you are finished, write your final draft on a separate sheet of lined paper.

LESSON 10
AUDIENCE

 **Lesson**

As with speaking, when writing we must choose the content and tone with our audience in mind. You wouldn't talk to your teacher the same way you talk to your friends. You probably wouldn't talk about the same things, either.

Picture this example: Rita is 12 years old and in the sixth grade. On Sunday she went to the mall with her friends. When she returned home she called her best friend, Maria, who was sick at home. Here is what she said about going to the mall.

"Oh my gosh, Maria, I saw the coolest hair clips with these butterflies on them and an awesome bracelet with hearts and butterflies and rainbows and unicorns. And oh my gosh, you'll never believe what Kimi told me..."

The next day at school, Rita's teacher Mr. Jackson asked the class to write a paragraph about something interesting they did over the weekend. Here is Rita's paragraph.

This weekend I went to the mall with my freinds. We looked at jewelry, clothes, and hairclips. Later, we each bought a slurpee and talked about music and movies. At 5:00 p.m. my Dad picked us up and drove us home. When I got home, I called my friend Maria who was sick at home. I told her all about the mall so she wouldn't feel left out.

Rita took one event and told it two different ways. Her tone was very excited when she spoke to Maria, but it was very factual when she wrote her paragraph for Mr. Jackson. Rita considered her audience before retelling her story.

Activity One

Read each item and answer carefully.

1. Your teacher tells you to write about the cheetah. After you finish your essay you will be reading it to a class of first graders.

    A. Who is your audience?

    B. X out the words you would not use in your essay.
cat	sub-saharan	hunter
spotted	quick	pounce
species	agile	cub

    C. How long should it take to read your essay to the class?
    30 seconds   5-7 minutes   30 minutes
    Why?

    D. Put a star next to the topics that would be appropriate for a class of first graders. Explain your answers.

    Why the cheetah is so fast.

    What the cheetah looks like.

    How cheetahs hunt and devour their prey.

    Shanta: The cheetah that saved a little girl's life.

2. Next you are assigned to write about bicycle safety. Which of the following audiences would be interested in the topic?
Circle your answers.

   School aged children

   The Society of Retired Astronauts

   Cat Lovers of America

   Parents for Safety

3. Which of the following topics would be appropriate for people living in Florida. Explain your answers.

   Dolphins: Our friends from the Ocean

   The damaging effects of sunburns

   Ice fishing

   Eliminating Massachusetts Turnpike tolls

4. Read the following paragraph then write 2-4 audiences that would be interested in reading it. Explain your answers.

Volunteer work benefits the community and the workers. Volunteer workers donate their time and skills in order to help a cause. These workers might deliver meals to people, run errands in hospitals, or build and repair parks and other public works. Other volunteers might visit the elderly or coach disabled children. Young people who volunteer might learn what profession they want to enter when they are older. Volunteering is an effective way to learn and apply skills while helping people.

Activity Two

It is important to know the audience you are writing for so you can attract their interest and give them useful information. Use the following exercises to learn how to think about different audiences.

EXAMPLE: Association of Fly Fisherman

>**Who are they?** people interested in fly fishing
>
>**What do they do?** fly fish
>
>**Where do they do this?** rivers and lakes
>
>**When do they do this?** in spare time, during good weather.
>
>**How do they do this?** with fly fishing equipment
>
>**Why do they do this?** for fun and relaxation

1. Society of Volunteer Firemen

Who are they? _____

What do they do? _____

Where do they do this? _____

When do they do this? _____

How do they do this? _____

Why do they do this? _____

2. Kids for the Environment

Who are they? _____

_____

What do they do? _____

_____

Where do they do this? _____

_____

When do they do this? _____

_____

How do they do this? _____

_____

Why do they do this? _____

_____

3. Dog Lovers of America

Who are they? _____

_____

What do they do? _____

_____

Where do they do this? _____

_____

When do they do this? _____

_____

How do they do this? _____

_____

Why do they do this? _____

_____

Journal Entry

Write an informative paragraph about a group or an organization to which you belong. Begin by describing your audience. Then follow all the informative paragraph steps from Lesson 9 using the templates in the back of your book to plan your paragraph. Finally, write the final draft on the lines below.

Audience:

Paragraph:

LESSON 11
ORGANIZING AND WRITING AN INFORMATIVE ESSAY

 **Lesson**

In Lesson 9 you learned to write an informative paragraph. Now you will learn to expand your ideas to the length of an essay. Just as you did with the informative paragraph, you need to brainstorm ideas.

Step 1: Brainstorm
Web

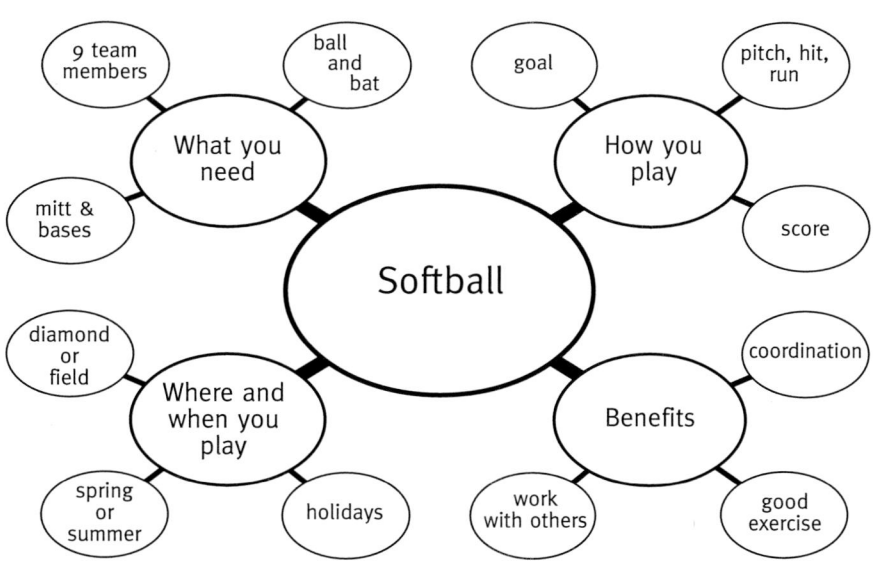

In Lesson 9 you brainstormed a number of ideas for your informative paragraph. However, you only focused on one brainstorming topic. With an informative essay you can include more or all of your brainstorming topics.

The next step is to group and sequence your brainstormed ideas from Lesson 9. The ideas from the softball web in Lesson 9 are grouped and ordered below.

Step 2: Group and Sequence Your Ideas

1. What you need. Where and When it is played.
2. How to play. Goal of the game.
3. Who plays. Benefits.

What is needed to play softball and where and when it is played should begin the essay, because they are important to know before learning how to play the game.
Next, the goal of the game is important, because the reader needs to understand the purpose of the game.
Finally, once the reader understands the game, it makes sense to take it further and discuss who plays and the benefits of playing.

You want to make sure that your grouping makes sense and that the order or sequence is logical.

 ## Activity One

Try writing your ideas on cards and rearranging the order until it sounds right. Then list the order below.

1. _____

2. _____

3. _____

4. (Optional) _____

Step 3: Outline

Next, you need to outline your ideas and think about some important details. What you see next is an outline that will help you to organize your essay and expand your ideas.
Notice how the softball paragraph is expanded.

Introductory Paragraph

Topic Sentence: Softball is a fun and interesting sport

What Will Reader Learn: How to play, the benefits of playing

Why Does Reader Want to Know: May want to play

Detail Paragraph 1   (first, one)

Topic Sentence: In spring and summer, outdoor sports such as softball are fun ways to enjoy the time of year.

Detail: 9 team members, softball, bat, mitt, bases

Detail: a diamond or any open field

Detail: warm spring or summer day

Example: Memorial day, 4th of July, Labor Day

Transitional Sentence: A few friends, nice weather, and some basic equipment are all you need to get started and have fun.

Detail Paragraph 2 (second, next, another)

Topic Sentence: Softball is not difficult to learn

_____

Detail: goal to have most runs in 7 innings

Detail: pitch ball, hit ball, run bases

Detail: score point at home plate

Example: _____

Transitional Sentence: _____

_____

Detail Paragraph 3 (third, also, in addition)

Topic Sentence: There are many benefits to playing softball.

_____

Detail: work with others

Detail: coordination

Detail: good exercise

Example: first year pitching

Transitional Sentence: The best part of playing is making friends

and meeting new people

Last Detail Paragraph   (last, finally)

Topic Sentence: _____

_____

_____

Detail: _____

Detail: _____

Detail: _____

Example: _____

Transitional Sentence: _____

_____

_____

Final Paragraph

Conclusion/Clincher: Softball is fairly easy so players can have loads of fun. _____

_____

Personal Thought: Great for everyone

_____

_____

Call to action: Join a team today

_____

_____

Notice the three elements in the **introductory paragraph**:
   the topic sentence;
   what the reader will learn;
   and why it is important or interesting.

The three **detail paragraphs** support the introductory paragraph by giving more information about the game of softball. Notice too how **examples** can help you get your point across. Not every paragraph needs an example, but try to include at least two in your essay.

The **transition sentences** conclude each paragraph and prepare the reader for what comes next. However, if you decide to use the transition words at the beginning of each paragraph, you don't always need to write transitional sentences.

The **conclusion** is the last paragraph. It includes:
   the **clincher sentence**;
   your **personal thoughts**;
   and a **call to action**.
The call to action is what you would like to see the reader do or how you want the reader to respond after reading the essay.

Activity Two

Now it is your turn to outline an informative essay. Turn to the next page and use your brainstorm from Lesson 9 to fill in the outline. Be sure to think about each prompt and try to generate examples to illustrate your ideas.

Introductory Paragraph

Topic Sentence: _____

_____

_____

What Will Reader Learn: _____

_____

_____

Why Does Reader Want to Know: _____

_____

_____

_____

Detail Paragraph 1   (first, one)

Topic Sentence: _____

_____

_____

Detail: _____

Detail: _____

Detail: _____

Example: _____

Transitional Sentence: _____

_____

Detail Paragraph 2 (second, next, another)

Topic Sentence: _____
_____
_____

Detail: _____

Detail: _____

Detail: _____

Example: _____

Transitional Sentence: _____
_____

Detail Paragraph 3 (third, also, in addition)

Topic Sentence: _____
_____
_____

Detail: _____

Detail: _____

Detail: _____

Example: _____

Transitional Sentence: _____
_____

Last Detail Paragraph   (last, finally)

Topic Sentence: _____

_____

_____

Detail: _____

Detail: _____

Detail: _____

Example: _____

Transitional Sentence: _____

_____

Final Paragraph

Conclusion/Clincher: _____

_____

_____

Personal Thought: _____

_____

_____

Call to Action: _____

_____

_____

Step 4: Write a Rough Draft

    Softball is a fun and interesting sport. To really enjoy the game of softball, you need to understand how it is played and the benefits of this sport. It is a good idea to learn these things if you are interested in playing softball.

    In spring or summer, when the weather turns nice, outdoor sports, such as softball, are fun ways to enjoy the time of year. Softball is played on a diamond or in an open field. Four real softball bases or any other markers, such as bags or flattened boxes, can be used to create the diamond. Each team needs nine members, mitts for each team member, a few bats, and a couple of large softballs. A few friends, nice weather, and some basic equipment is all you need to get started and have fun.

    Softball is not difficult to learn. The ball is pitched from the pitcher's mound, either slow or fast. The batter waits until the ball begins to pass over home plate then swings the bat. After she hits the ball, the batter tries to get around as many bases as possible. Every time a player gets back to home plate, the team scores a point. The goal of the game is to get the most players around the bases in 7 innings, and the team with the most points at the end wins.

    There are many benefits to playing softball. First, you learn how to work with others to benefit the whole team. Softball is a team sport so you should always think about what is best for the team, not just what is best for you. Second, playing softball can help you become more coordinated. For example, my first year pitching I went from throwing lots of balls to throwing mostly strikes by the end of the season. Finally, softball provides you with good exercise which is important for staying healthy.

    The best part of playing softball is spending time with friends and meeting people. Families, church groups, and summer campers are just a few of the people who enjoy the game of softball.

    Softball is a fairly easy sport to play so the players can have loads of fun. I think it is a great sport for people of all ages. So if you want to have fun, meet new people, and get great exercise, join a softball team today.

Activity Three

Now it is your turn to write your rough draft. When you are finished use the editing guidelines in the back of your book to help you edit your essay. Then on a separate piece of lined paper, write a final draft.

Step 5: Edit

After writing your rough draft, you should reread your paragraph a few times looking for errors. Look for the following types of errors:
- capitalization
- punctuation
- spelling
- subject/verb agreement
- run-on sentences
- incomplete sentences

Step 6: Final Draft

On a separate piece of lined paper, write your final draft.

LESSON 12
SEQUENCING INFORMATION

 **Lesson**

Different types of paragraphs and essays need different methods for sequencing information. Sequencing means to put things in order.

General to Specific: This is the method of ordering information that you have used so far in writing informative paragraphs and essays. You begin with a topic sentence which states your general statement. Then you give reasons, specific examples, facts, or other detail to support the general statement.

Chronological Order: When we put things in chronological order, we put them in the order that they happened.
One place we use chronological order is in narrative writing. In Book One you used the transition words—*first, next, then, after that,* and *finally* to help you sequence the events in your stories.
We can also use chronological order in expository writing. You may want to write about a special event, such as winning a track meet or an event in history.

 **Activity One**

On Thursday morning, Mrs. Rosenberg was walking her dog, Fifi, when she witnessed a small car accident. She was asked to give a report of what she saw to the police. The following sentences are from her report. Put the sentences in chronological order by numbering them 1 to 5.

_____ The green car was in front of the yellow car.

_____ The yellow car slammed on its brakes, but it was too late. He hit the green car.

_____ I was walking my dog along the lake.

_____ The man in the yellow car was talking on his phone.

_____ The green car turned on its blinker and slowed.

Now combine the sentences using the transition words—*first, next, then, after that,* and *finally* to create an informative chronological paragraph. Elaborate on the details if you wish. Don't forget to include a topic sentence and a conclusion.

Order of Location: Another way to sequence information is by the order of location. This is often done when describing a person, place, or thing. Location words such as *above, below, next to, beside, north, south, east, west, left, right* are used to tell the location of features you are describing.

*My favorite place to be is my bedroom. I like to lie on my bed, which is **beneath** the window. The sunlight streams in casting its warm rays into the **center** of my room. I reach to my **right** and flip on the radio that sits **atop** my night stand. My favorite music fills the room and I snuggle in a blanket and look **up** at my ceiling from which a color mobile of the solar system hangs. My eyes wander over to the bookshelf, **opposite** my bed and I read a few titles deciding on a new book to read. Then I remember the new library book I brought home. I look around the room trying to remember where I put it. Finally my eyes move to the **left** of the bookshelf and there it is peeking out **beneath** a stack of homework papers. I get the book, knowing I should do homework instead. I lie down on my bed again, open the book, and enter another world. Homework can wait.*

Notice the bolded location words. They help the reader picture where things are in the room and the movements of the central character. Without strong location words, the reader would have a difficult time picturing the story.

Activity Two

Listed below are some sentences describing certain people, places, and things. Put the sentences in order from 1 to 5. Then see if you can guess the person, place, or thing (hint: when describing an animal or person it is a good idea to go from top to bottom). While you read each item, underline the location words to help you picture.

_____The males have tusks which protrude from beneath the nose.

_____This animal has two large ears on the sides of its head.

_____This animal has four legs beneath its enormous gray body.

_____Its hind tail hangs from the top of its back to the middle of its legs.

_____It has a long nose which can move flexibly from left to right or up and down.

What animal are you picturing?

_____Its right arm is extended upward holding a torch.

_____This American landmark is on the east coast.

_____Its feet stand upon a concrete foundation on an island.

_____A crown sits atop its head.

_____A gown hangs from its shoulder to the ground.

What landmark are you picturing?

_____He was often found in the White House.

_____He wore black pants over his gangly legs.

_____Long thin arms hung next to his body.

_____He had a dark beard.

_____A tall black hat was often seen on his head.

Who are you picturing? (hint: We celebrate his birthday in February.)

Order of Importance: A third way to sequence information is by order of importance. Let's say you are writing a list of things you need to do. You might start by listing the most important things first, that way if you don't finish the list, at least you accomplished the most important ones. In a paragraph or essay about a person, you may want to start with his/her most important accomplishment in order to interest the reader right away. Other times, you may want to start with the least important information, because it may be odd or attention getting and also quickly interest the reader.

> *Abraham Lincoln was one of the most remarkable presidents. Perhaps his greatest achievement was the Emancipation Proclamation which abolished slavery, freeing thousands of slaves. Before his presidency, Lincoln was a small town lawyer and state congressman who boldly spoke out against slavery. Though plagued with bouts of depression, Lincoln never gave up hope that one day all men, black and white, would be free. This belief in freedom led him into politics and eventually to the White House. Lincoln's contributions to the people of the United States have made our country a better place to live.*

Now read the next paragraph which puts the same information in reverse order, from the least to the most important.

> *Abraham Lincoln made remarkable contributions to the United States. Though plagued with bouts of depression, Lincoln never gave up hope that one day all men, black and white, would be freemen. As a small town lawyer and state congressman, Lincoln boldly spoke out against slavery. This belief in freedom led him into politics and eventually to the White House. As President of the United States, Lincoln achieved perhaps his greatest accomplishment, the Emancipation Proclamation. This historic document abolished slavery, freeing thousands of slaves. By sticking to his convictions, Lincoln helped to make the United States a better and stronger country.*

Both paragraphs are equally effective in informing the reader of Lincoln's contributions to the United States.

Activity Three

Read the following paragraphs and decide whether they begin with the most important or the least important information.

    Meriwether Lewis and William Clark were men of adventure, courage, and honor. In 1801, Lewis was asked by President Thomas Jefferson to lead a 40 man expedition to discover the Northwest Passage, a water route from St. Louis, Missouri to the Pacific Ocean. Lewis and Clark and their crew survived two years of extreme weather, rough terrain, and near starvation. Yet they never faltered in their courage and goals. Although they did not find a direct water route to the Pacific Ocean, they did make it to the coast and back, documenting plants, animals, and Native American tribes unknown to Americans. It was Lewis and Clark who opened the western part of the United States and began the tide of westward expansion.

    Cesar Chavez was a poor immigrant who dedicated his life to improving the conditions of farm workers. As late as the 1980's farm workers were subject to harsh conditions and very low wages. They moved from farm to farm picking crops, often living in one room shacks with no electricity or plumbing. Children of farm workers rarely went to school and few were able to learn English and improve their status. Chavez organized the farm workers into a successful union that could strike for better pay, equal treatment, and improved working conditions. Today, Chavez is a hero among farm workers.

    The most damaging hurricane in United States history was Hurricane Andrew in 1992. The hurricane brought structural and economic devastation to Southern Florida and Louisiana. Total damage was estimated at 25 billion dollars, making it the most expensive natural disaster in United States history. Andrew was categorized as a level 4 hurricane with violent winds reaching 145 mph. Despite its destructiveness, Andrew killed only 15 people. Yet close to a quarter million people were left temporarily homeless. Today meteorologists are working to better predict and warn people of approaching hurricanes in order to save people the grief of such devastating natural disasters.

Activity Four

The following outline includes a topic sentence, three details, and a conclusion. Put the details in order of importance, from the most to the least important, and write a paragraph on the lines that follow.

Topic Sentence: Fresh fruits and vegetables are tasty and healthy snacks.

Detail: delicious, inexpensive and easy to find

Detail: help you fight illness

Detail: vegetables have vitamins and minerals

Detail: fruit salad healthy alternative to sugary snacks

Conclusion: Eat fruits and vegetables to satisfy your taste buds and keep your body healthy.

_____
_____
_____
_____
_____
_____
_____
_____
_____
_____
_____
_____
_____

There are two more ways to order information: **Step by Step** order which we will discuss in the next lesson, Writing an Operational Paragraph, and **Compare/Contrast** which we will discuss in Lessons 19 and 21.

Journal Entry

Pick a topic from the back of your book and write a paragraph or essay. Before you begin, write one sentence stating who your audience is and another sentence stating which method of ordering details you are using.

Audience: _____

_____

_____

_____

Method of sequencing: _____

_____

_____

Paragraph/Essay

_____

_____

_____

_____

_____

_____

_____

_____

_____

_____

_____

LESSONS 9-12
CUMULATIVE REVIEW

Take this cumulative review test to make sure you understand the lessons you have learned. If you miss items on the test, go back and review the lessons you had difficulty with, or do the comprehensive exercises in the back of your book.

1. What is a topic sentence?
   _____
   _____

2. What are the three parts of an informative paragraph?
   _____
   _____

3. You are asked to write a paper for the school drama club. Which two topics would interest your audience?
   Training Your Dog to do Tricks
   Projecting Your Voice on Stage
   Ways to Memorize Your Lines
   Litter Removal

4. If you were to read an essay to a second grade class, about how long should it take?

   90 seconds   4-6 minutes   25 minutes

5. In an informative essay, roughly how many examples should you include?
   _____
   _____

6. What three things are included in a closing paragraph?

_____

_____

7. _____ order sequences information in the order that it happened.

8. Use words such as *above, below, next to, beside, north, south,* etc. when sequencing information by order of _____.

9. When sequencing information by the order of importance you:

    A. Should always start with the most important detail
    B. Should always start with the least important detail
    C. May start with either the least or most important detail

LESSON 13
OPERATIONAL PARAGRAPHS

 **Lesson**

Sometimes we want our paragraph or essay to explain how to do something. This is called an **operational** paragraph.

In an **operational** paragraph, it is important that you give the steps in the exact order they need to be done. It is also important that your directions are clear and understandable to the reader.

When planning your paragraph or essay try to think of every single step, no matter how small. Never assume your reader will already know something. As with informative paragraphs and essays, start by brainstorming. In an operational paragraph you need to think about the following:
- —the purpose of the paragraph
- —what the reader needs to know
- —what is needed
- —the steps in the process

Look below at the brainstorm for how to make a peanut butter and jelly sandwich.

Step 1: Brainstorm

Purpose: To make a peanut butter and jelly sandwich

reader needs to know	materials	steps
what a sandwich is	2 slices of bread	gather ingredients
what each of the ingredients are	peanut butter	smear peanut butter
	jelly	smear jelly
	knife	put together
	plate	clean up

If the reader already knows what a sandwich is and what each of the ingredients are, then your audience is probably American or Canadian, since most other countries don't have peanut butter. Usually kids eat peanut butter and jelly, so your audience is probably a North American kid. Your audience would not be a Japanese exchange student, because he or she would not be familiar with peanut butter and jelly.

Activity One

Now it is your turn to brainstorm. You will be writing about how to ride a bike safely. Your audience will be the kids in your school.

Purpose:

reader needs to know   materials   steps

Once you have brainstormed your ideas, it is time to organize your paragraph. Remember that sequencing is very important and in an operational paragraph we organize in a step by step sequence. You must organize in the exact order that the steps are done. For example, you don't want to tell someone to put the two slices of bread together before they have smeared on the peanut butter and jelly.
You also need to generate a topic sentence and a conclusion/clincher sentence.

Step 2: Outline

Notice that you might have four or five steps. Less steps may mean that you forgot a step. More steps may cause the reader to get lost in the process.

Topic Sentence/Main Idea
If you need a little snack after school, try making a peanut butter and jelly sandwich.

What you need

need 2 slices of bread, peanut butter, jelly, a knife, a plate

Step One (first)

smear peanut butter on one slice

Step Two (second, then)

smear jelly on other slice

Step Three (third, next)

put slices together

Final Step (last, finally)

clean up your mess

Conclusion

enjoy your sandwich

Activity Two

Now it is your turn to write an outline. Use the outline template below. After you outline your ideas, write a rough draft using complete sentences and the transition words provided.

Topic Sentence/Main Idea

What you need

Step One   (first)

Step Two   (second, then)

Writing Adventures Book 2

Step Three (third, next)

_____

_____

Step Four (fourth, after that)

_____

_____

Final Step (last, finally)

_____

_____

Conclusion

_____

_____

Step 3: Rough Draft

Write a rough draft of your bicycle safety paragraph on the lines below.

_____
_____
_____
_____
_____
_____
_____
_____
_____
_____
_____
_____
_____
_____
_____
_____
_____
_____

Step 4: Edit

Now reread your paragraph a few times looking for errors. Remember to look for the following types of errors:

- capitalization
- spelling
- run-on sentences
- punctuation
- subject/verb agreement
- incomplete sentences

Step 5: Rewrite-Final Draft

Once you edit your mistakes, write a final draft on a separate piece of lined paper.

LESSON 14
OPERATIONAL ESSAY

 **Lesson**

Now you are going to take your operational paragraph and expand it. Remember, the first step to writing an essay is brainstorming. We will be using the ideas from the operational paragraph brainstorm in Lesson 13. However, this time the audience will be a Japanese exchange student. Therefore, we will need to go into more detail.

Step 1: Brainstorm

Purpose: To make a peanut butter and jelly sandwich

reader needs to know	materials	steps
what a sandwich is	2 slices of bread	gather ingredients
what each of the ingredients are	peanut butter	smear peanut butter
	jelly	smear jelly
	knife	put together
	plate	clean up

When you elaborate on a step, think about *why* and *how* to do the step.

EXAMPLE: Step 1: Use a knife to smear peanut butter on one slice.

   Elaborate: How — spread evenly over whole slice

   Why — get peanut butter in every bite

You also want to think about defining the materials that may be unknown to the Japanese student.

EXAMPLE: Peanut butter is pureed peanuts. You can buy it at any American grocery store.

Now look at the outline below. Notice how each step will become a paragraph, and the why and how of each step is explained to give more information to the reader.

Step 2: Outline

Introductory Paragraph

Topic Sentence: If you need a little snack after school, try making a peanut butter and jelly sandwich.

Why: Healthy snack that will help you think in order to finish your homework.

What You Need: 2 slices of bread, peanut butter (pureed peanuts), jelly (sweetened and cooked fruit), knife, plate

Transitional Sentence: Now you are ready to begin.

Step 1 Paragraph (first)

Topic Sentence: Use a knife to smear peanut butter on one slice of bread.

How: lots of peanut butter, evenly

Why: get peanut butter in every bite

Step 2 Paragraph   (second, then)

Topic Sentence: use knife to smear jelly on the other slice.

How: don't use too much jelly, evenly

Why: don't want jelly to squirt out

Step 3 Paragraph   (third, next)

Topic Sentence: Put slices together so peanut butter and jelly meet in the middle.

How: with clean sides on the outside

Why: don't get hands dirty

Last Step Paragraph   (last, finally)

Topic Sentence: be sure to clean up your mess.

How: put everything away, wash dishes, wipe counter

Why: so mom doesn't get mad

Final Paragraph

Conclusion/Clincher: _Now you can enjoy your sandwich._

Personal Thought: _best way to pick up your energy for homework._
and play.

Call to Action: _Eat up!_

Notice the three elements in the **introductory paragraph**:
    the **topic sentence**;
    what you need;
    and a **transitional sentence**. A transitional sentence leads the reader from the introduction into the first step of the process.

The **steps** all include the how and why.

The **conclusion** is the last paragraph. It includes:
    your **clincher sentence**;
    your **personal thoughts**;
    and a **call to action**.

Activity One

Use the outline below to organize your operational essay. Remember to use your brainstorming ideas on bicycle safety from Lesson 13. Also remember that your audience is now a Japanese exchange student.

Introductory Paragraph

Topic Sentence: _____

_____

_____

Why: _____

_____

What You Need: _____

_____

_____

Transitional Sentence: _____

_____

_____

Step 1 Paragraph   (first)

Topic Sentence: _____

_____

_____

How: _____

Why: _____

Step 2 Paragraph   (second, then)

Topic Sentence: _____

_____

_____

How: _____

Why: _____

Step 3 Paragraph   (third, next)

Topic Sentence: _____

_____

_____

How: _____

Why: _____

Last Step Paragraph   (last, finally)

Topic Sentence: _____

_____

_____

How: _____

Why: _____

Final Paragraph

Conclusion/Clincher: _____

_____

_____

Personal Thought: _____

_____

_____

Call to Action: _____

_____

_____

After you outline your ideas, you are ready to write your rough draft.
    You will now have a five or six paragraph essay.
    Indent the first word in each paragraph.

Step 3: Rough Draft

If you need a little snack after school, try making a peanut butter and jelly sandwich. It is a healthy snack with a lot of protein that will help you to think and finish your homework. This snack may be unusual in your country, but I'm sure it will be an instant hit with all the kids.

To make a peanut butter and jelly sandwich you will need: two slices of bread; peanut butter, which is a common American food item made from pureed peanuts; jelly, which is cooked and sweetened fruit preserves; a knife; and a plate. Once you have these, you are ready to begin.

First, use a knife to smear peanut butter on one side of one slice of bread. Be sure to use plenty of peanut butter and spread it evenly over the slice of bread. This will allow you to get peanut butter in every bite.

Second, use the knife to smear jelly on one side of the other slice of bread. Be sure you don't use too much jelly or it will squirt out when you eat the sandwich.

Third, put the slices of bread together so the peanut butter and jelly meet in the middle. This allows the peanut butter and jelly to mix together. The outside of a sandwich is the clean sides of bread, so your hands won't get dirty.

Finally, be sure to clean up your mess. Put everything away, wash your dishes, and wipe off the kitchen counter. Regardless of what country you come from, moms get mad when you leave a mess.

Now you can enjoy your all-American peanut butter and jelly sandwich. I think this is the best way to pick up your energy for homework and play. Share a sandwich with a friend and start a delicious trend in your country today. Eat up!

Step 4: Edit

After you write your rough draft, reread it a few times looking for errors. Remember to look for the following types of errors:

- -capitalization
- -spelling
- -run-on sentences
- -punctuation
- -subject/verb agreement
- -incomplete sentences

Step 5: Rewrite—Final Draft

Now it's your turn to write your final draft on a separate piece of lined paper.

LESSON 15
FINDING YOUR VOICE AND POINT OF VIEW

 **Lesson**

Write Honestly and Sincerely
Writing is much like talking. Some people talk slowly and deliberately. Others talk quickly and exuberantly. The way we talk says a lot about who we are. Regardless of our style, when we talk honestly and sincerely about subjects we are truly interested in, people tend to listen. It is the same with writing. If you choose a subject you are truly interested in and write honestly and sincerely, people will want to read your work.

"Talk" to the Reader
Use your own voice when writing and pretend as if you are having a conversation with someone about your topic. "Talk" to your audience and write freely. Try to include personal experiences to back up or illustrate your facts. Think of your audience and try to relate your essay to their everyday experiences.

Feel Good About Your Writing
Feel good about the content and your choice of words. If you are satisfied with what you wrote, chances are your reader will be too.

Stick with a Single Point of View
Most writers use either the first-person or third-person point of view. **First-Person Point of View** is when the writer gives a straight forward account of the facts from his or her own perspective. The author will use first person pronouns such as *I, me*, and *my*. First-person is often used in narrative writing, when the author is one of the characters. It can be used in expository writing, especially in persuasive essays. However, most expository writing is done in the third-person point of view.

Third Person Point of View is when the writer does not use the pronouns *I, me, my*. The writer is coming from an observational or authority point of view.

EXAMPLE: First Person: I enjoy skiing and ice skating in winter.

Third Person: Winter is a good time to enjoy skiing and ice skating.

Activity One

Decide if each sentence is written from the **first person** or **third person** point of view.

EXAMPLE: *Mom baked a cake for Dad.* Third-Person

1. Yo Yo Ma is a well known cello player.

2. My friends came to my house to play darts.

3. The pencil sharpener broke.

4. Magnolias are the first flowers to bloom in spring.

5. When visiting New York City, I always go to the Museum of Natural History.

6. Our alarm clock failed to go off and we were late for school.

7. Dairy is one of the main food groups in good nutrition.

8. Maya Angelou is my favorite poet.

9. Last summer, I went to an amusement park and rode the roller coaster.

10. My dream vacation would be to visit Hawaii.

11. Mom went to the store to get some milk.

12. Niagra Falls is a popular tourist site.

13. At my Dad's office, I played on his computer.

14. The pear is a tasty fruit.

15. My Grandmother was a hula-hoop champion.

Activity Two

The following paragraph is written from the **first-person** point of view. Rewrite it in the **third-person**. This is good practice for editing expository pieces that should be written in the third-person.

When I am looking for a summer job, I follow a few specific steps. First, I look through a newspaper and find a job opening that interests me. I also make sure that I have the skills required for the job. Second, I contact the employer and request an appointment to fill out an application and be interviewed. When I prepare for the interview, I dress for success so I feel confident. Finally, I arrive at the appointment on time and with all the information needed to complete the application. By following these steps, I am sure to find a fulfilling summer job.

Journal Entry

Journal Entries are always written from the first-person point of view. On the lines below, write about your biggest pet peeve. A pet peeve is something that bothers you. For example, a pet peeve might be people biting their fingernails.

LESSON 16
ORGANIZING AND WRITING A PERSUASIVE PARAGRAPH

 Lesson

Sometimes the purpose of a paragraph or essay is to persuade or convince the reader to believe or act in a certain way.
For example, you may want to persuade someone to buy your bicycle or persuade your classmates to vote for you for class president.
As with the other paragraphs and essays you have written, you need to begin with brainstorming. We will use the same brainstorm web that was used with informative paragraphs. Below you see a brainstorm for persuading someone to buy a bicycle.

Step 1: Brainstorm

Web

- buy my bike
  - quality
    - top of the line
    - excellent condition
  - features
    - 15 speeds
    - new tires
    - on & off road
  - cost
    - $75
  - popular

The writer thought of many reasons someone should buy his bike. Not all are good reasons. For example, no one will buy a bike just because the seller needs the money. The next step is to choose the most convincing reasons to buy the bike.

Step 2: Choose the Most Convincing Reasons/Argument

 ## Activity One

Now it is your turn to brainstorm ideas for your persuasive paragraph. Your topic will be **why your classmates should vote for you for class president.**

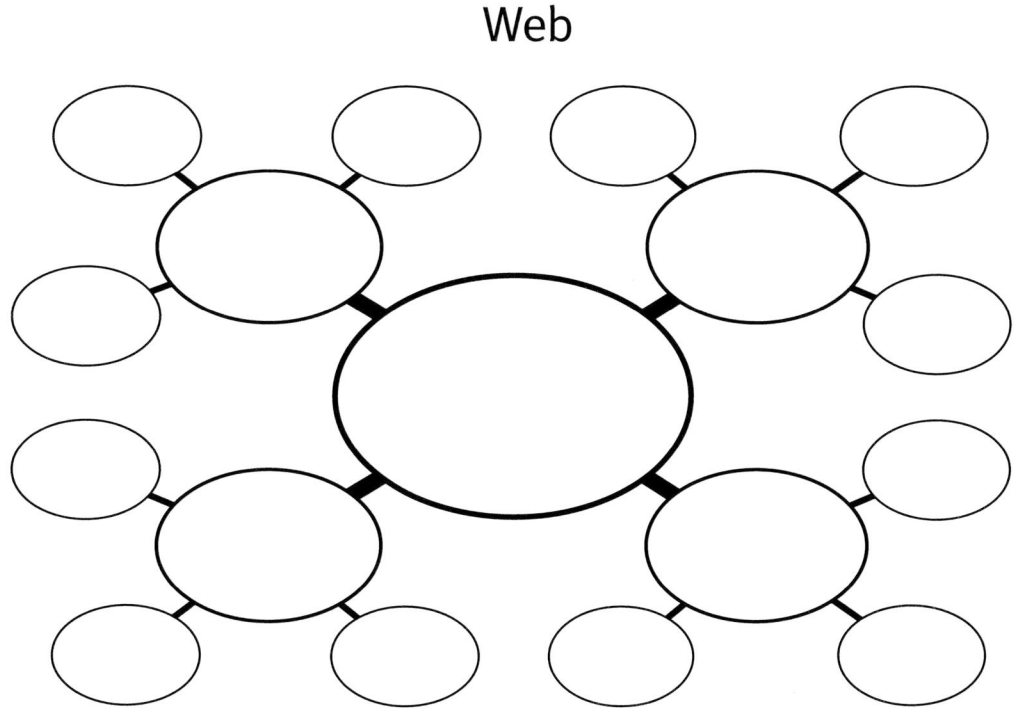

Web

 ## Activity Two

Think about each argument in your brainstorm and ask yourself if it is a convincing reason why you should be class president. Cross out any arguments you think are not convincing.

Next, you need to organize your argument using an outline. Notice how the outline prompts you for the audience. This is very important in persuasive paragraphs and essays. This writer is writing for an ad in a newspaper. The outline helps you to construct a good argument. In this case, an argument is not bickering between two people. An argument is more like a case a lawyer would present to persuade a judge or jury.

Step 3: Outline

Topic: Buy my bicycle.   **Audience:** Newspaper Ad

Topic Sentence/Main Idea

Want a new bike? You better act now or this great deal with be gone.

Detail Sentence   (the first reason)

top-of-the-line, excellent condition

Detail Sentence   (another reason, secondly)

15 speeds, new tires

Detail Sentence   (as well, furthermore)

popular

| Detail Sentence | (last, finally) |

only $75

_____

_____

| Conclusion Sentence |

Deals like this happen once in a lifetime

_____

_____

In the **Topic sentence/main idea** the writer used the adjective "great" to make the bike attractive to the reader right away. He also made the matter seem urgent — they would be missing a good opportunity.

> **Topic Sentence:** States what the writer wants the reader to believe or how the writer wants the reader to act.

The **details** support the argument by giving positive reasons for buying the bike. The writer never mentioned anything negative, because he wants the reader to only imagine how great the bike is. Also notice the words in parentheses. These are transition words you should use to introduce each new detail.

> **Details:** The reasons the reader should believe your argument.

The **conclusion** had the same sense of urgency and missed opportunity that the topic sentence had.

> **Conclusion/Clincher:** Restates what the writer wants the reader to believe or do.

Activity Three

Outline your paragraph using the outline below.

Topic: Vote for class president   **Audience:** Classmates

Topic Sentence/Main Idea

Detail Sentence	(the first reason)

Detail Sentence	(another reason, secondly)

Detail Sentence	(as well, further more)

Detail Sentence	(last, finally)

Conclusion Sentence

After you outline your ideas, you are ready to write a rough draft. Here are a few things to remember:

    Indent the first word in a paragraph.

    Turn your main idea, each detail, and the conclusion into complete sentences.

    Use transition words.

Step 4: Rough Draft

Want a new bike? You better act now or this great opportunity will be gone. The first reason you should buy my bike is that it is a top-of-the-line mountain bike and is in excellent condition. Secondly, it has 15 speeds and new tires which will allow you to ride on or off the road. Furthermore, my bike is the most popular brand among kids today. Finally, and most enticing, is the low, low price of only $75. So don't hesitate. Deals like this happen only once in a lifetime.

Activity Four

Now it is your turn to write a rough draft on a separate piece of lined paper. You should try to do your best, but remember this is a rough draft. You will edit and revise your work before writing the final draft.

Step 5: Edit

After writing your rough draft, you should reread your paragraph a few times looking for errors. Look for the following types of errors:

- capitalization
- punctuation
- spelling
- subject/verb agreement
- run-on sentences
- incomplete sentences

Step 6: Rewrite-Final Draft

Once you edit your mistakes, write a final draft on a separate piece of lined paper.

LESSON 17
ORGANIZING AND WRITING A PERSUASIVE ESSAY

 **Lesson**

In the last lesson you learned to write a persuasive paragraph. Now you will learn to expand your ideas to the length of an essay. Just as you did with the persuasive paragraph, you need to brainstorm ideas. We will be using the same ideas for the persuasive essay.

Step 1: Brainstorm

Web

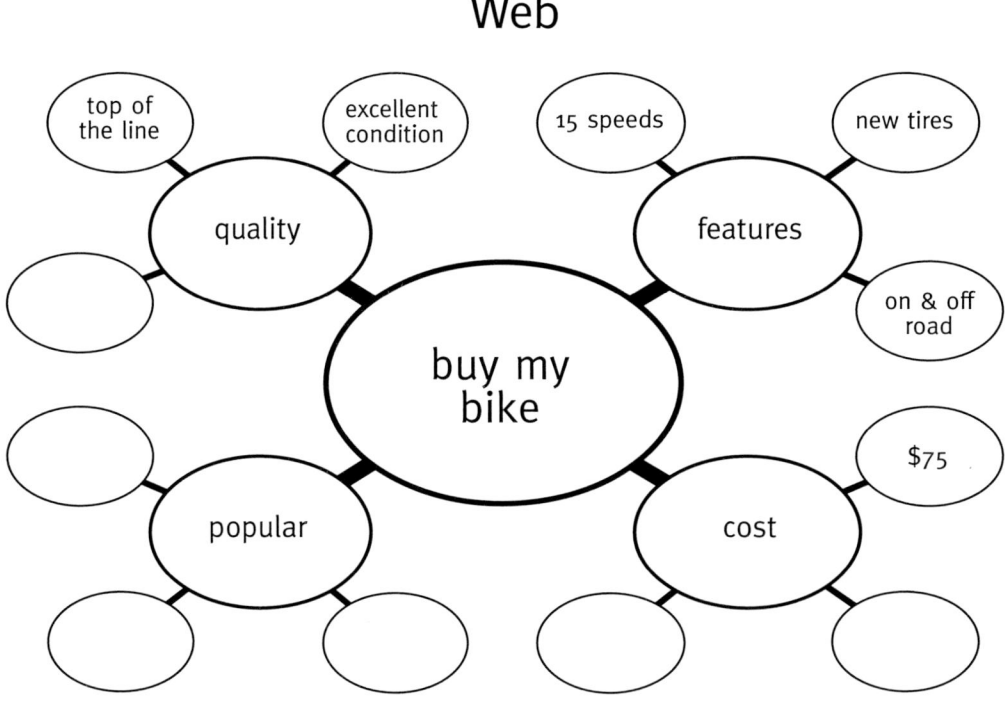

Next you need to organize your ideas and expand the support of your argument. What you see next is an outline that will help you to organize your essay and expand your ideas. Notice how we take the bike paragraph and expand it.

Step 2: Outline

Introductory Paragraph

Topic Sentence: Want a new bike? You better act now or this great deal will be gone.

Summarize the Details: top-of-the-line, experts agree, missed opportunity

Transitional Sentence: Here are a few good reasons to buy my bike.

Paragraph 1 – Give the Facts

Topic Sentence: You won't find a quality bike like this anywhere.

Fact: 15 speeds and new tires

Fact: excellent condition

Fact: only $75

Transitional Sentence: Don't take my word for it.

Paragraph 2 – Refer to an Expert

Topic Sentence: Joe Smith, owner of Bike World, agrees that my bike is a great deal

Quote from Expert: "The owner takes excellent care of it. I could sell it for 3 times as much."

Transitional Sentence: With an expert opinion like that it's a wonder that anyone would disagree.

Paragraph 3 – Answer the Opposition

Topic Sentence: Don't listen to the scooter crowd.

What the Opposition Says: some people say that mountain bikes are out and scooters are in.

Refute the Opposition: mountains, dirt, faster, paper route

Transitional Sentence: A mountain bike can make getting around fast and easy.

Paragraph 4 – State Likely Consequences

Topic Sentence: Once in a lifetime opportunity

Consequence: will pay a lot more

Consequence: will regret it

Consequence: _____

Transitional Sentence: _____

Final Paragraph

Conclusion/Clincher: What are you waiting for?

Personal Thought: I'd call immediately and get it.

Call to Action: Act now.

Notice the three elements in the **introductory paragraph**: the **topic sentence, summary of details,** and a **transitional sentence.**

The **detail paragraphs** support the introductory paragraph in four different ways.

1. **giving the facts** — these are positive facts about the bike that will make the reader want to buy it. Notice how it is basically the paragraph from lesson 16.
2. **referring to an expert** — an expert is someone who knows a lot about the subject, in this case bikes.
   For practice you can make up an expert, but when you are writing a real essay you should personally ask an expert or research an expert in the library or on the internet.
3. **answering the opposition** — not everyone will agree with your opinion. Predict some likely arguments against your opinion and defend your ideas.
4. **stating the consequences** — state what is likely to happen if the reader does not believe or act the way you want them to.

The **conclusion** is the last paragraph. It includes your **clincher sentence,** your **personal thoughts,** and a **call to action.** The call to action is what you would like to see the reader do or how you want the reader to respond after reading the essay.

Activity One

Use the outline on the following pages to expand your paragraph on running for class president. When you get to the expert opinion, think of something your parents or friends would say about why you would make a good class president.

Introductory Paragraph

Topic Sentence: _____

_____

_____

Summarize the Details: _____

_____

_____

Transitional Sentence: _____

_____

_____

Paragraph 1 – Give the Facts

Topic Sentence: _____

_____

_____

Fact: _____

Fact: _____

Fact: _____

Transitional Sentence: _____

_____

_____

Paragraph 2 – Refer to an Expert

Topic Sentence: _____
_____
_____

Quote from Expert: _____
_____
_____

Transitional Sentence: _____
_____
_____

Paragraph 3 – Answer the Opposition

Topic Sentence: _____
_____
_____

What the Opposition Says: _____
_____

Refute the Opposition: _____
_____

Transitional Sentence: _____
_____
_____

Paragraph 4 – State Likely Consequences

Topic Sentence: _____

_____

_____

Consequence: _____

Consequence: _____

Consequence: _____

Transitional Sentence: _____

_____

_____

Final Paragraph

Conclusion/Clincher: _____

_____

_____

Personal Thought: _____

_____

_____

Call to Action: _____

_____

_____

After you outline your ideas, you are ready to write a rough draft on a separate sheet of lined paper. You will now have a five or six paragraph essay. Indent the first word in each paragraph.

Step 3: Rough Draft

Want a new bike? You better act now or this great deal will be gone. Experts agree that this top-of-the-line mountain bike won't be around long and you could miss this excellent opportunity. Here are a few of the reasons you should buy this bike.

You won't find a quality bike like this anywhere else. The bike is in excellent condition. It has 15 speeds and new tires, which will allow you to ride it on or off the road. Whats more, it is only $75.

Don't just take my word for it. Joe Smith, owner of Bike World, says that this bike is a top-of-the-line mountain bike. "The owner takes excellent care of it. I could sell it in my shop for three times as much," Smith says. With an expert opinion like this it's a wonder anyone would disagree.

Some people say that mountain bikes are out and scooters are in. Well, you can't ride a scooter up and down mountains and along dirt trails. And if you need to get somewhere fast, a scooter can't do the job, but a mountain bike can. Furthermore, it would be very difficult to do a paper route on a scooter. A mountain bike can make getting around fast and easy.

Last, I'd just like to say that this is truly a once in a lifetime opportunity. If you don't act now, you will end up paying a lot more for a new bike. You'll wish you had taken me up on this great offer.

What are you waiting for? Act now. If I were you, I'd call immediately and come right over and snatch up this mountain bike before the rest of town is beating down the door to buy it.

Step 4: Edit

After you write your rough draft, reread it a few times looking for errors. Remember to look for the following types of errors:

- -capitalization   -punctuation
- -spelling   -subject/verb agreement
- -run-on sentences   -incomplete sentences

Step 5: Rewrite-Final Draft

Then on a separate sheet of lined paper, write your final draft.

LESSONS 13-17
CUMULATIVE REVIEW

Take this cumulative review test to make sure you understand the lessons you have learned. If you miss items on the test, go back and review the lessons you had difficulty with, or do the comprehensive exercises in the back of your book.

1. What type of paragraph or essay explains how to do something?

   _____
   _____

2. What four things should you think about when brainstorming for an operational paragraph or essay?

   _____
   _____

3. When writing an operational essay, each step should explain _____ and _____ each step is done.

4. When an author writes from the first person point of view, what three pronouns might he use?

   _____
   _____

5. When an author writes from an observational or authority point of view it is called _____ person point of view.

6. What type of paragraph or essay tries to convince the reader to believe or act in a certain way?

   _____
   _____

7. When writing a persuasive paragraph or essay, your details should give _____ the reader should believe your argument.

8. In a persuasive essay you need to:
   give the _____   refer to an _____
   answer the _____   state likely _____

LESSON 18
STYLISTIC OPENERS

 **Lesson**

Good writing will grab the reader's attention immediately. The best writers in the world are known for their opening sentences or paragraphs. Read the following opening sentence from the novel, *Bridge to Terabithia*, by Katherine Paterson.

> *Ba-room, ba-room, ba-room, baripity, baripity, baripity, baripity—Good. His dad had the pickup going.*

The words of this opening sentence immediately capture the readers attention because they are the sounds of an old truck starting. This is called onomatopoeia. A big word that is hard to pronounce, but the point is that it works to get the readers attention and that is what you want to do with your opening sentences.

Stylizing opening sentences takes a lot of practice and experimentation. Certainly Katherine Paterson wrote several drafts of this opening sentence, before finally feeling satisfied that it would capture her readers. There are a number of ways to stylize your opening sentences.

Tell a funny story

EXAMPLE: They say Maniac Magee was born in a dump.
They say his stomach was a cereal box and
his heart a sofa spring.

—From *Maniac Magee*, by Jerry Spinelli

State a startling fact
The 1906 San Francisco Earthquake set off numerous fires, destroyed hundreds of buildings, and killed over 3,000 people.

Pose a question
Have you ever wondered what happens to a falling star?

Make a confession
I have to admit, slipping that frog into Mrs. Green's purse wasn't the best idea.

Use a famous quotation
"I have a dream." Those famous words spoken by Martin Luther King still inspire us today.

Begin with dialogue
"Do not enter," the strange voice boomed as I stepped before the golden pyramid.

Flashback with a story
I remember that hot, humid summer day three years ago when I sat sulkily in my hammock nursing my broken arm.

Activity One

Read the following opening lines and determine which stylistic opener is being used.

1. Did you ever have one of those days where everything seemed to go wrong?

   _____

2. There's no doubt about it. I'm definitely the worst player on the team.

   _____

3. "Don't make me say it again, Trevor," my mother roared up the stairs.

   _____

4. Despite the ferocity of the tornado, there was only one casualty of the disaster, old man McAlister's cow, Bessie.

5. "Four score and seven years ago...," Abraham Lincoln began as he delivered the Gettysburg Address in November of 1863.

6. At 10:00pm on October 17, in the middle of a dust wheat field, the metallic ship landed with stealth silence.

7. "I'm never going back to school," I yelled, slamming my bedroom door.

8. Have you ever had one of those days when you just want to lay on the couch and have your mom feed you chicken soup even though you're not sick?

9. "Give me liberty or give me death..."

10. Every year over 10,000 Americans die from the effects of illegal drug use.

Activity Two

Go back to your informative paragraph in Lesson 9 and write a stylistic opener by stating a unique or startling fact about your favorite animal.

_____
_____
_____
_____
_____
_____
_____
_____
_____
_____

Go back to your operational paragraph in Lesson 13 and write a stylistic opener by making a confession.

_____
_____
_____
_____
_____
_____
_____
_____
_____
_____

Go back to your persuasive paragraph in Lesson 16 and write a stylistic opener by posing a question or two.

LESSON 19
COMPARE & CONTRAST PARAGRAPHS

 **Lesson**

A comparison paragraph discusses the **similarities** between people, places, ideas, and so on.
A contrast paragraph discusses the **differences** between people, places, ideas, and so on.
Two subjects can be similar or different in appearance, personality, function, talent, likes and dislikes, and many other ways.

Step 1: Brainstorm

Brainstorming using a Venn diagram helps you to think about and list the similarities and differences between your subjects.

EXAMPLE: Similarities and differences between dogs and cats

Compare / Contrast

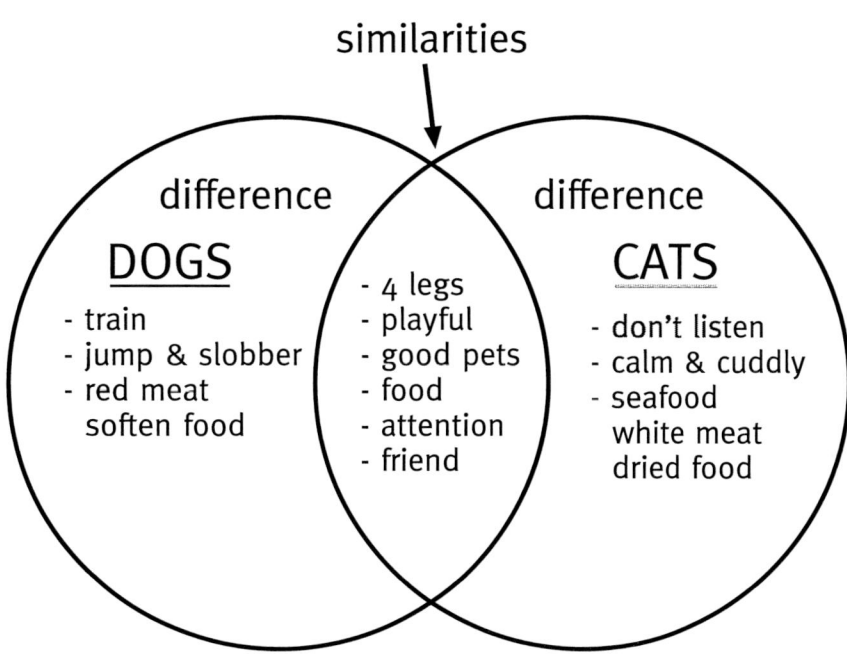

Activity One

Now it is your turn to brainstorm similarities and differences for your topic.

Topic: The personalities of you and your best friend.

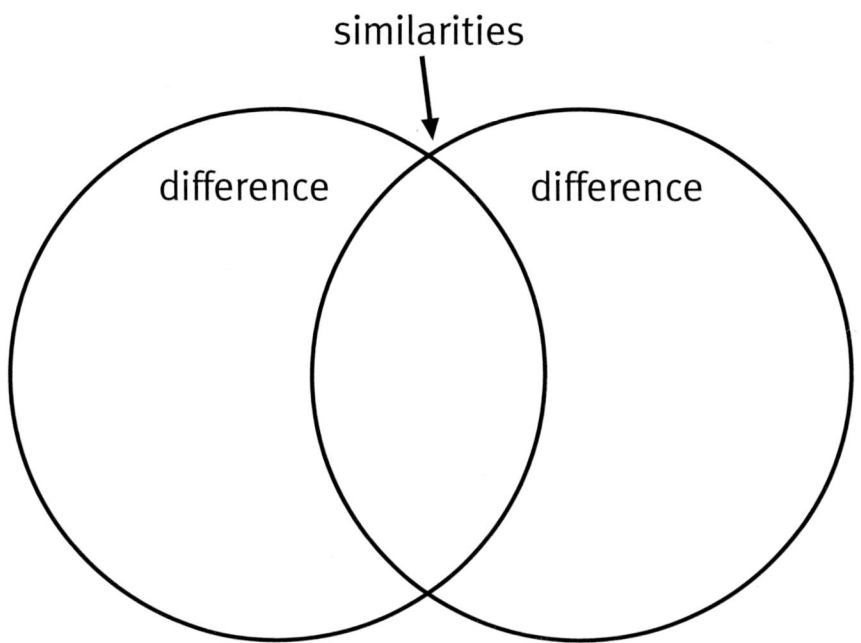

After brainstorming, you are ready to outline your paragraph. You may use all or only some of your brainstorming ideas. Let's start with a comparison paragraph.

Step 2: Outline

Notice that some ideas were grouped together according to **appearance** (legs, fur, tail, paws), **personality** (playful, good pets), **needs** (feed, attention) and so on.
Also notice that not every idea was used. The writer chose what he thought was important.

Topic Sentence/Main Idea

Dogs and cats have some similar characteristics

Detail Sentence (one way)

4 legs, fur, tails, paws

Detail Sentence (also)

playful, make good pets

Detail Sentence (in addition)

need you to feed and pay attention

Detail Sentence (last, finally)

like always having a friend

Conclusion Sentence

With so many things in common, it may be difficult to choose which pet you want.

Activity Two

Use the outline below to organize your paragraph. Categorize your similarities by appearance, personality, likes and dislikes, talents, and one other category of your choice.

Topic Sentence/Main Idea
_____
_____

Detail Sentence   (one way)
_____
_____

Detail Sentence   (also)
_____
_____

Detail Sentence   (in addition)
_____
_____

Detail Sentence   (last, finally)
_____
_____
_____

Conclusion Sentence
_____
_____
_____

After you outline your ideas, you are ready to write a rough draft. Here are a few things to remember:

    Indent the first word in a paragraph.

    Turn your main idea, each detail, and the conclusion into complete sentences.

    Use transition words.

Step 3: Rough Draft

Dogs and cats have some similar characteristics. One way they are alike is that they both have four legs, fur, a tail, and paws. Also, both are playful and make good pets. In addition, dogs and cats need you to feed them and pay attention to them. Finally, they are similar in that they make you feel like you always have a good friend. With so many things in common, it may be difficult to choose which pet you want.

 **Activity Three**

Now it is your turn to write a rough draft. You should try to do your best, but remember this is a rough draft. You will edit and revise your work before writing the final draft.

Step 4: Edit

After writing your rough draft, you should reread your paragraph a few times looking for errors. Look for the following types of errors:
- capitalization
- spelling
- run-on sentences
- punctuation
- subject/verb agreement
- incomplete sentences

Step 5: Rewrite-Final Draft

Once you edit your mistakes, write a final draft on your journal entry page.

Contrast Paragraph

Now we are going to use the differences between cats and dogs to write a contrast paragraph. We can use the Venn diagram brainstorm to write a contrast paragraph as well.

Step 1: Brainstorm

Compare / Contrast

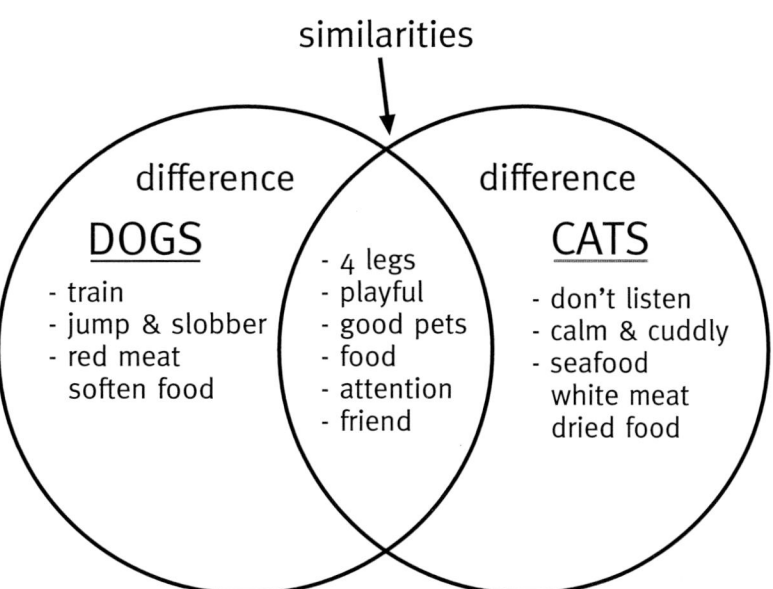

Take a look at the following outline. Notice that the transition words allow the writer to go back and forth between both subjects.

Step 2: Outline

Topic Sentence/Main Idea

While dogs and cats both make good pets, there are differences between them.

Detail Sentence (Subject One)   (first of all)

dogs: train tricks

Detail Sentence (Subject Two)   (on the other hand)

cats, refuse to listen

Detail Sentence (Subject One)   (secondly)

dogs: jump and slobber

Detail Sentence (Subject Two)   (however)

cats, calm and cuddly

Detail Sentence (Subject One)   (finally)

dogs: red meat, soften food

> **Detail Sentence** (Subject Two)   (in contrast)
>
> cats, seafood, white meat, dried food

> **Conclusion Sentence**
>
> So you can see there are differences between dogs and cats
>
> that you may want to think about before selecting a pet.

Notice that we go back and forth between subject one (dogs) and subject two (cats). The idea is to state a fact about subject one and then show how subject two is different. The transition words are very important cues to the reader. They make it clear that you are contrasting the two subjects. There are additional transition words listed in the back of your book.

Also, ideas are grouped by **categories**— talents, personality, and food preferences.

Activity Four

Use the ideas in your Venn diagram on the differences in personality between you and your best friend to complete the outline below. Remember to group details in categories. For this paragraph, group by personality, talents, and likes and dislikes.

Topic Sentence/Main Idea
_____
_____

Detail Sentence (Subject One)   (first of all)
_____
_____

Detail Sentence (Subject Two)   (on the other hand)
_____
_____

Detail Sentence (Subject One)   (secondly)
_____
_____

Detail Sentence (Subject Two)   (however)
_____
_____

Detail Sentence (Subject One)   (finally)
_____
_____

```
┌─────────────────────────────────────────────────────┐
│ Conclusion Sentence                                 │
│ _____ │
│ _____ │
└─────────────────────────────────────────────────────┘

┌─────────────────────────────────────────────────────┐
│ Detail Sentence (Subject Two)    (in contrast)      │
│ _____ │
│ _____ │
└─────────────────────────────────────────────────────┘
```

After you outline your ideas, you are ready to write a rough draft. Here are a few things to remember:

Indent the first word in a paragraph.
Turn your main idea, each detail, and the conclusion into their own complete sentence.
Use transition words.

Step 3: Rough Draft

While dogs and cats both make good pets, there are differences between them. First of all, dogs can be trained to do tricks such as fetching a stick or rolling over. On the other hand, cats refuse to listen and do whatever they want. Secondly, dogs tend to get really excited and jump up and slobber all over you. Cats, however, are calm and don't slobber. They are also more cuddly. Finally, dogs and cats eat different food. Dogs like red meat and their dried food must be moistened. In contrast, cats eat more white meat such as seafood, chicken, and turkey. Also they like their dried food crunchy. So you can see there are differences between dogs and cats that may help you decide which pet is best for you.

Activity Five

Write a rough draft of your contrast paragraph on the lines below.

Step 4: Edit

After writing your rough draft, you should reread your paragraph a few times looking for errors. Look for the following types of errors:
- capitalization
- spelling
- run-on sentences
- punctuation
- subject/verb agreement
- incomplete sentences

Step 5: Rewrite-Final Draft

Once you edit your mistakes, write the final draft of your contrast paragraph after the final draft of your comparison paragraph on a separate sheet of lined paper.

LESSON 20
SENSORY, MEMORY, & REFLECTIVE DETAIL

 **Lesson**

You have written a few paragraphs and essays now and have generated several details about your subjects. Most of your details are considered **personal details,** those which you gathered based upon your personal experiences either through your senses, memories, or imagination. **Sensory details** are those which you perceive through your own senses (sight, smell, touch, hearing, and taste).

> **EXAMPLE:** *The sweet smell of the red rose hit me as I reached to touch the velvety softness of the petals.*

Your senses told you that the smell was sweet and that the petals felt soft.

Memory details are those from your own past experiences.

> **EXAMPLE:** *Lying in my hospital bed, the beautiful bouquet lifted my spirits and eased the ache of my broken leg. I knew then that the people who loved me would always be there for me.*

You remembered that event in order to tell it.

Reflective details are those you try to predict by imagining what would have been or what you hope might happen.

> **EXAMPLE:** *What sorrow I would have felt, had no one been there to show me love and cheer me up.*

You had to imagine the opposite of how you really felt.

Activity One

Think of your favorite stuffed animal or toy from when you were 4 or 5 years old. Next to each sense, list as many words or phrases you can think of to describe your toy. Then write a sentence using some of your sensory details.

Name of Toy:

Sight:

Smell:

Touch:

Hearing:

Taste:

_____
_____
_____
_____
_____
_____

 **Activity Two**

Listed below are different nouns that you are probably familiar with. For each noun fill in the sensory, memory, and reflective detail from your experiences or your imagination.

EXAMPLE: Swimming pool

Sensory: exhilarating, cool, refreshing

Memory: During my first swim meet, the exhilarating water motivated me to be a strong swimmer and win the race.

Reflective: If I had not joined the swim team, I would not have met my best friend Frank.

1. Shark

Sensory: _____

Memory: _____

_____

Reflective: _____

_____

2. Rain drops

Sensory: _____

Memory: _____

_____

Reflective: _____

_____

3. Freshly baked cookies

Sensory: _____

Memory: _____

_____

Reflective: _____

_____

4. Baseball bat

Sensory: _____

Memory: _____

_____

Reflective: _____

_____

5. Sand

Sensory: _____

Memory: _____

_____

Reflective: _____

_____

6. Wrapped gift

Sensory: _____

Memory: _____

_____

Reflective: _____

_____

7. Puppy

Sensory: _____

Memory: _____

_____

Reflective: _____

_____

8. Flower field

Sensory: _____

Memory: _____

_____

Reflective: _____

_____

9. Airplane flight

Sensory: _____

Memory: _____

_____

Reflective: _____

_____

10. Amusement park ride

Sensory: _____

Memory: _____

_____

Reflective: _____

_____

Activity Three

We also use sensory, memory, and reflective detail to describe events. The following paragraph contains such details. Underline each detail and above the detail write whether it is sensory, memory, or reflective.

Graduation day was finally here. The sun was warm and glowing over the spring lawn filled with families and friends. Looking back, it was a perfect day. I can remember feeling nothing but pride for the hard work and perseverence I had dedicated to my studies during the past four years. In my hands the diploma felt crisp. As I spotted my family in the boisterous crowd, I knew their support would always follow me. How lucky I felt to know that others believed in me as I believed in myself.

Activity Four

Write a sentence or two about a memory you have of a pet. Then write a sentence predicting how you would have felt without that pet.

_____
_____
_____
_____
_____
_____
_____
_____
_____

 **Activity Five**

Write a paragraph about your pet using sensory, memory, and reflective details.

 **Journal Entry**

Look around your room and find an object that is special to you. On a separate sheet of lined paper, write a paragraph about that object. Include sensory, memory, and reflective detail. In your paragraph describe what the object is, when and where you received it, why it is special, and how it will affect you in the future. Use an informative paragraph brainstorm and outline to help you generate and organize your ideas.

LESSON 21

ORGANIZING AND WRITING COMPARE & CONTRAST ESSAYS

Lesson

In this lesson, you will learn to expand a comparison or contrast paragraph into a longer essay.

First you need to brainstorm using a Venn Diagram. Look back at the Venn Diagram you used to brainstorm your ideas in Lesson 19. See if you can think of any more details you would like to add. Then return to this page to learn how to outline your ideas.

Step 1: Brainstorm

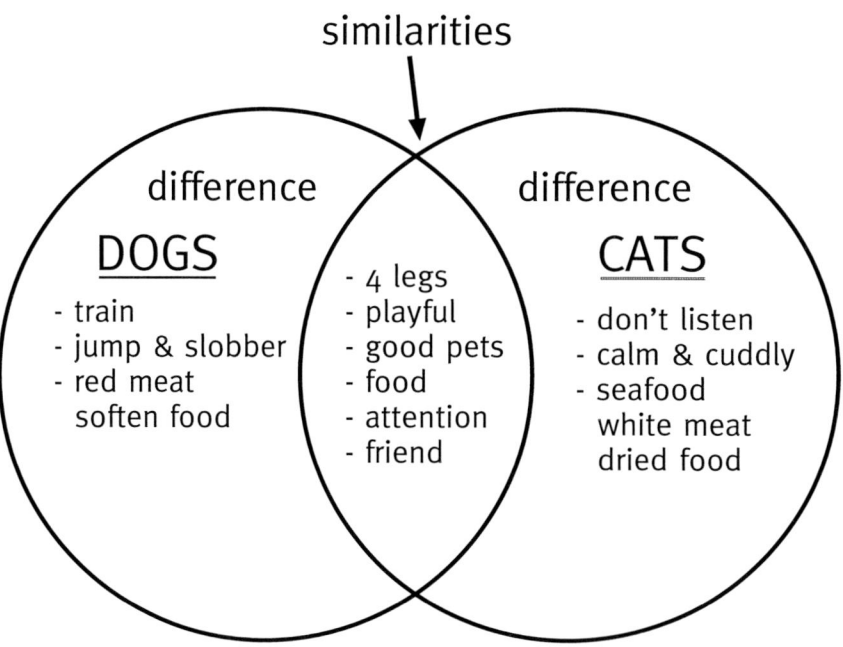

The next step is to outline your ideas.
The following example is an expanded comparison paragraph.
Notice that the outline elaborates on each detail.

Step 2: Outline

Introductory Paragraph

Topic Sentence: Dogs and cats have some similar characteristics.

Summarize the Details: appearance and personality

Why Does Reader Want to Know: May help decide which pet to get

---

Detail Paragraph 1 (one way)

Topic Sentence: Dogs and cats have similar features

Detail: 4 legs, fur, a tail, and paws

Elaborate: short or long fur, swish tails, rough pads

Transitional Sentence: These animals love to get excited and play

Detail Paragraph 2 (also)

Topic Sentence: Dogs and cats are playful and make good pets.

Detail: chase, wrestle

Elaborate: friendly, loyal, loving

Transitional Sentence: As long as you take care of them

Detail Paragraph 3 (in addition)

Topic Sentence: Dogs and cats both need to be fed and need attention.

Detail: food and water and attention

Elaborate: feed once in morning and once at night

Transitional Sentence: They will also give love back.

Last Detail Paragraph   (last, finally)

Topic Sentence: Dogs and cats make good friends.

Detail: someone to play with and talk to

Elaborate: hug and a kiss

Transitional Sentence: They are both so irresistible.

Final Paragraph

Conclusion/Clincher: You can see that dogs and cats share many common traits

Personal Thought: I had a difficult time choosing so I have both.

Call to Action: get a pet today

Notice the three elements in the **introductory paragraph**:
- the **topic sentence**;
- **summary of details**;
- and a **transitional sentence**.

The **detail paragraphs** support the introductory paragraph and elaborate on each detail.

The **conclusion** is the last paragraph. It includes:
- your **clincher sentence**;
- your **personal thoughts**;
- and a **call to action**.

Activity One

Now it is your turn to outline a comparative essay, using the outline template below.

Introductory Paragraph

Topic Sentence: _____

_____

_____

Summarize the Details: _____

_____

_____

Why Does Reader Want to Know: _____

_____

_____

Detail Paragraph 1 (one way)

Topic Sentence: _____

_____

_____

Detail: _____

Elaborate: _____

_____

_____

Transitional Sentence: _____

_____

Detail Paragraph 2 (also, another way)

Topic Sentence: _____

_____

_____

Detail: _____

Elaborate: _____

_____

_____

Transitional Sentence: _____

_____

Detail Paragraph 3   (in addition)

Topic Sentence: _____

_____

_____

Detail: _____

Elaborate: _____

_____

_____

Transitional Sentence: _____

_____

Last Detail Paragraph   (last, finally)

Topic Sentence: _____

_____

_____

Detail: _____

Elaborate: _____

_____

_____

Transitional Sentence: _____

_____

Final Paragraph

Conclusion/Clincher: _____

_____

_____

Personal Thought: _____

_____

_____

Call to Action: _____

_____

_____

After you outline your ideas, you are ready to write a rough draft of your essay.

You will now have a five or six paragraph essay.

Indent the first word in each paragraph.

Step 3: Rough Draft

Dogs and cats have some similar characteristics. They are somewhat similar in appearance, as well as personality. Their common characteristics can make it difficult to choose which pet you would like to have.

One way these animals are similar is in their physical features. Dogs and cats both have 4 legs, fur, a tail, and paws. Their fur can be short or long. As well, both have rough pads that protect their paws. Dogs and cats both swish their tails when they are excited. These animals love to get excited and play.

Dogs and cats are also playful and make good pets. Both like to chase things and playfully wrestle with humans. Furthermore, they both make good pets because they are friendly, loyal, and loving. That is, as long as you take care of them.

Both dogs and cats need to be fed, and they need attention. Dogs and cats need special food and plenty of water. You should feed them once in the morning and once in the evening. On top of needing food, they need attention and love from the humans they live with. They also give love back.

Dogs and cats make good friends. When you have one as a pet you will always have someone to play with and talk to. Also, if you're feeling down, they are always there to give you a hug and a kiss. They are both so irresistible.

You can see that dogs and cats share many common traits. This can make it difficult to choose which pet to take home. Personally, I had a difficult time choosing so I have both a dog and a cat. It's wonderful having pets. So if you don't have one, get a pet today. You won't regret it.

 Activity Two

Write a rough draft of your essay on a separate sheet of lined paper.

Step 4: Edit

Now reread your paragraph a few times looking for errors. Remember to look for the following types of errors:

-capitalization -punctuation
-spelling -subject/verb agreement
-run-on sentences -incomplete sentences.

Step 5: Rewrite-Final Draft

Once you edit your mistakes, write a final draft on a separate sheet of lined paper.

Contrast Essay

Now you will learn to expand a contrast paragraph into a longer essay.

Step 1: Brainstorm

Again, you will elaborate on your ideas from your contrast paragraph.

Introductory Paragraph

Topic Sentence: While dogs and cats both make good pets, there are some differences between them.

Summarize the Details: talents, personality, likes and dislikes

Why Does Reader Want to Know: help you decide on a pet

Detail Paragraph 1 (Subject One)   (first of all)

Topic Sentence: dogs can be trained

Detail: fetch, walk, tricks

Elaborate: fetch stick, bones, or balls. Sit, stand, roll over, frisbee

Transitional Sentence: These abilities are unique to dogs.

Detail Paragraph 2 (Subject Two)   (on the other hand)

Topic Sentence: Cats don't listen.

Detail: minds of their own

Elaborate: can jump, but only when they want to

Transitional Sentence:

Detail Paragraph 3 (Subject One)   (secondly)

Topic Sentence: Dogs can get very excited and jump and slobber all over you.

Detail: excited to see you

Elaborate: wag tails and run around until they get attention

Transitional Sentence: Crave attention because they are so loving.

Detail Paragraph 4 (Subject Two)　　　(however)

Topic Sentence: Cats are generally calm and don't slobber. _____

_____

_____

Detail: act like they don't care _____

Elaborate: may punish you for being gone _____

_____

_____

Transitional Sentence: Yet, cats can be very cuddly, curling up

　　at your feet to sleep the days and nights away. _____

Detail Paragraph 5 (Subject One)　　　(last, finally)

Topic Sentence: Dogs and cats differ in what they like to eat. _____

_____

_____

Detail: red meat _____

Elaborate: my dog likes his food moistened _____

_____

_____

Transitional Sentence: _____

_____

Detail Paragraph 6 (Subject Two)   (in contrast)

Topic Sentence: cats prefer white meat.

Detail: chicken, turkey, and seafood

Elaborate: My cat likes her dried food crunchy not moist.

Transitional Sentence:

Final Paragraph

Conclusion/Clincher: You can see there are differences between dogs and cats that you may want to consider before taking one home.

Personal Thought: I like having one of each.

Call to Action: get a pet today

 Notice in the example an expanded contrast paragraph.

Step 2: Outline

Introductory Paragraph

Topic Sentence: _____
_____
_____

Summarize the Details: _____
_____
_____

Why Does Reader Want to Know: _____
_____
_____

Detail Paragraph 1 (Subject One)   (first of all)

Topic Sentence: _____
_____
_____

Detail: _____

Elaborate: _____
_____
_____

Transitional Sentence: _____
_____

Detail Paragraph 2 (Subject Two)   (on the other hand)

Topic Sentence: _____
_____
_____

Detail: _____

Elaborate: _____
_____
_____

Transitional Sentence: _____
_____

Detail Paragraph 3 (Subject One)   (secondly)

Topic Sentence: _____
_____
_____

Detail: _____

Elaborate: _____
_____
_____

Transitional Sentence: _____
_____

Detail Paragraph 4 (Subject Two)   (however)

Topic Sentence: _____
_____
_____

Detail: _____

Elaborate: _____
_____
_____

Transitional Sentence: _____
_____

Detail Paragraph 5 (Subject One)   (last, finally)

Topic Sentence: _____
_____
_____

Detail: _____

Elaborate: _____
_____
_____

Transitional Sentence: _____
_____

Detail Paragraph 6 (Subject Two)   (in contrast)

Topic Sentence: _____

_____

_____

Detail: _____

Elaborate: _____

_____

_____

Transitional Sentence: _____

_____

Final Paragraph

Conclusion/Clincher: _____

_____

_____

Personal Thought: _____

_____

_____

Call to Action: _____

_____

_____

Activity One

Complete the outline below for a contrast essay.

Step 3: Rough Draft

While dogs and cats both make good pets, there are some differences between them. They differ in talents, personality, and likes and dislikes. Once you read about how dogs and cats differ, you will be ready to decide which pet is best for you.

First of all, dogs can be trained to do tricks. They can fetch sticks, bones, or tennis balls. Dogs can learn to walk, sit, stand, or rollover on command. Dogs are good at playing frisbee. They run and jump to catch the frisbee. These abilities are unique to dogs.

On the other hand, cats do not listen to training. They can play fetch but only when they feel like it. Cats will never walk, sit, stand, or rollover when you want them to. They really have minds of their own. Cats are able to jump very high or jump down from tall places without hurting themselves. However, they'll only jump when it suits them.

Secondly, dogs can get very excited and jump and slobber all over you. As soon as you get home they start running around wagging their tails just waiting for a big hug and slobbery kiss. They crave attention so much because they are so loving.

However, cats are generally calm and don't slobber. Cats act as if they don't care whether you are home or not. In fact, they may even punish you for being out by biting or scratching you when you get home. Yet, cats can be very cuddly, curling up at your feet to sleep the days and nights away.

Finally, dogs and cats differ in what they like to eat. Dogs like red meat. Being related to coyotes and wolves, dogs prey on other animals. However, domesticated dogs usually just prey on a can of dog food. My dog also likes dried food, but he prefers it moistened with water.

In contrast, cats prefer white meat. Cats generally prefer chicken and turkey and the liver and giblets that come with them. Seafood is also a favorite of cats. My cat likes her dried food crunchy instead of soft.

So you can see there are differences between dogs and cats that you may want to consider before taking one home. Personally, I have one of each—a dog to play with and a cat to cuddle. So if you don't have one, get a pet today. You won't regret it.

Activity Two

Write a rough draft of your contrast essay on a separate sheet of lined paper.

Step 4: Edit

Now reread your paragraph a few times looking for errors. Remember to look for the following types of errors:

- -capitalization
- -spelling
- -run-on sentences
- -punctuation
- -subject/verb agreement
- -incomplete sentences.

Step 5: Rewrite-Final Draft

Once you edit your mistakes, write a final draft on a separate sheet of lined paper.

LESSON 22
RUN-ON SENTENCES

 **Lesson**

Punctuation and connector words are very important. Without the correct words or punctuation the reader will get confused. The reader may also lose attention.

A **run-on sentence** is two or more complete thoughts joined without punctuation or connector words.

EXAMPLE: *Maria and her horse jumped over the gate they landed with grace.*

The sentence above has two complete thoughts — first, **Maria and her horse jumped** and second, **they landed**. So the sentence contains two subject/verb combinations, but does not contain punctuation or a connector word.

One way we can fix the sentence is with punctuation.

EXAMPLE: *Maria and her horse jumped over the gate. They landed with grace.*

We used a period to separate each complete thought, making each its own sentence.

Another way we can fix the sentence is with a connector word.

EXAMPLE: *Maria and her horse jumped over the gate and landed with grace.*

The connector "and" was used to connect the ideas. Notice that we removed the word "they" because we state the subjects, Maria and her horse, only once.

Activity One

Fix the run-on sentences using punctuation.

1. The school bell rang signaling the beginning of classes the children ran indoors.

2. The holiday traffic was heavy there were many small accidents on the road.

3. Mother went to the grocery store she bought my favorite snack.

4. The lights dimmed the audience grew quiet the orchestra began.

5. The tea kettle steamed and whistled Ann turned off the stove and poured the water in the teapot.

6. The rain pounded on the roof Gloria reached for her umbrella before leaving the house.

7. The plane pulled away from the gate it taxied to the runway.

8. The audience stood the president entered the room.

_____

_____

9. The children argued over the doll Mother took the doll away.

_____

_____

10. The ice cream dripped from the cone Josh licked the cone trying to get every bite.

_____

_____

Activity Two

Now fix the same run-on sentences using connector words and/or connecting punctuation. Try using the following connector words: *and, because, so,* and *as.* Also, think about which sentences sound best, those you created in Activity One or those created in Activity Two.

1. The school bell rang signaling the beginning of classes the children ran indoors.

_____

_____

2. The holiday traffic was heavy there were many small accidents on the road.

_____

_____

3. Mother went to the grocery store she bought my favorite snack.

_____

_____

4. The lights dimmed the audience grew quiet the orchestra began.

5. The tea kettle steamed and whistled Ann turned off the stove and poured the water in the teapot.

6. The rain pounded on the roof Gloria reached for her umbrella before leaving the house.

7. The plane pulled away from the gate it taxied to the runway.

8. The audience stood the president entered the room.

9. The children argued over the doll Mother took the doll away.

10. The ice cream dripped from the cone Josh licked the cone trying to get every bite.

# Activity Three

The following paragraphs each contain two run-on sentences. Underline the run-on sentences and write them correctly on the lines below.

    A warm summer day at a professional baseball game is good family fun. It is exciting to watch the pitchers throw the ball from the mound when the batters swing the crowd always anticipates contact and watches the ball to see if it sails into the stands. It is a good idea to bring a mitt in case you are lucky enough to catch a foul ball or a homer. Sometimes the batter will sign the ball for you after the game. The concession stands usually offer excellent hot dogs, fries, and ice cream souvenirs such as baseball hats and t-shirts can also be purchased. Whether your favorite team wins or loses, you still have a great time.

During the 1906 San Francisco Earthquake, my grandmother saved a handful of gold. At 8:56 am my grandmother's house on Fell Street began to shake quickly the tremors increased and things began to fall from the ceiling and the walls. Without thinking my grandmother and her 12 brothers and sisters ran from the house they looked back to see the roof catch fire. When the earthquake and aftershocks ended and the fire was put out, nothing remained but ashes. As my grandmother sifted through the rubble looking for mementos she uncovered a handful of Chilean gold coins, all that was left of her family's fortune.

Journal Entry

Ask your parents or grandparents to tell you about a memorable event in your family's history. On the lines below, write a paragraph or essay retelling the story. Use an informative brainstorm and outline to help you generate and organize your ideas. Also, use chronological sequencing when ordering your paragraph or essay.

LESSON 23

ORGANIZING AND WRITING A FORMAL LETTER

 **Lesson**

In this lesson, you will learn to write a formal letter.
A formal letter has the following components:

Heading: The heading includes the date, your name and address, and the name and address of the person you are writing to.

EXAMPLE: April 4, 2000
Lily Austin
4 Whiskers Avenue
Critterbury, MA 01010

Joe Lobster
6 Wharf Street
Seashore, MA 01011

Greeting: The greeting usually begins with "Dear" or "To Whom it May Concern".

EXAMPLE: Dear Mr. Lobster,

Body: The body of your letter should be organized like any other paragraph or essay. Your **topic sentence** should state why you are writing. The **details** should support the reason for your letter. Finally, the **conclusion** should close your letter by reminding the reader why you are writing.

EXAMPLE:

Topic Sentence: Myself and my fellow cats at the Cat Legion are working to end kitty hunger in Critterbury.

Detail: local business donations
Detail: feed stray cats 2 meals
Detail: cod, scrod, lobster, shrimp and salmon

Conclusion: Your support is appreciated.

Closing: Sign off with "Sincerely" or "Best Regards" and your name.

Signature: Finally handwrite your signature.

Here is how your letter should look when completed.

April 4, 2000

Lily Austin
4 Whiskers Avenue
Critterbury, MA 01010

Joe Lobster
6 Wharf Street
Seashore, MA 01011

Dear Mr. Lobster,

Members of the local Cat Legion are working to end kitty hunger in Critterbury. We are asking local businesses to donate generously to our Fish Drive For Hunger. We are hoping to feed stray cats two meals a day at our headquarters in the alley behind the fish market. Please let us know if you can donate any cod, scrod, lobster, shrimp, and especially salmon. Your support is appreciated.

Best Regards,

Lily Austin
President
Cat Legion 101

FORMAL LETTER OUTLINE

HEADING

Date:
_____

Your name & address:
_____
_____
_____

Name and address of the person you are writing to:
_____
_____
_____

GREETING

_____

BODY

Topic sentence: (Why you are writing the letter): _____
_____
Supporting detail: _____
Supporting detail: _____
Supporting detail: _____
Call to action: (How you want the reader to respond): _____
_____

CLOSING

_____

SIGNATURE

_____

 **Activity One**

Fill-in the missing components of the letter below. Refer to the outline on the previous page to guide you. Generate your own ideas. For example, the date can be any date you wish. (Hint: there are five missing components)

56 Appleturnover Circle
Pie Crust, WY 78678

Midwest Pie Contest

Mr. Peachcobbler,

    I am writing in regards to the rejection letter I received concerning my apple turnovers. I argue that a turnover should also be considered a pie. First, a pie consists of a crust and filling. A turnover also consists of crust and filling. Secondly, pies are baked at 375 degrees and are sliced into 8 servings. My apple turnovers are also baked at 375 degrees and can be sliced into 8 servings. Finally, like pies, apple turnovers can be served a la mode (with ice cream).

Sincerely,

Activity Two

Write the body for the following letters. Use the body outline from the Formal Letter Outline to help you organize your ideas. Also fill in your name and address in the appropriate space.

1. You have collected five box tops which are redeemable for a free watch. Write to the cereal company requesting your watch.

April 2, 2001

Crunchy Cereal Company
200 Branflakes Way
Shopee, NY 10234

To Whom it May Concern,

_____
_____
_____
_____
_____
_____
_____
_____

Sincerely,

2. The wheel on your new scooter broke. Write a letter to the manufacturer requesting a new wheel.

June 2, 2001

Scooters-A-Go-Go Inc.
Parts and Repairs Office
89798 Avenue B
Trend City, FL 40930

Dear Parts and Repairs Office,

_____
_____
_____
_____
_____
_____
_____
_____

Sincerely,

 **Journal Entry**

On the lines below, write a formal letter to your parents requesting a raise in your allowance. Follow the Formal Letter Outline.

LESSONS 18-23
CUMULATIVE REVIEW

Take this cumulative review test to make sure you understand the lessons you have learned. If you miss items on the test, go back and review the lessons you had difficulty with, or do the comprehensive exercises in the back of your book.

1. *The 1906 San Francisco Earthquake set off numerous fires, destroyed hundreds of buildings, and killed over 3,000 people.*

   The above sentence is an example of which type of stylistic opener?

   _____

   _____

2. *"I have a dream."*

   The above sentence is an example of which type of stylistic opener?

   _____

   _____

3. A comparison paragraph or essay discusses the _____ between people, places, ideas etc.

4. A contrast paragraph or essay discusses the _____ between people, places, ideas etc.

5. _____ details are those which you perceive through your own senses.

6. _____ details are those from your own past experiences.

7. _____ details are those you try to predict by imagining what would have been or what you hope might happen.

8. A _____ sentence is two complete thoughts joined without punctuation or connector words.

9. Fix the following run-on sentence using the connector word *as*.

The pianist played the final note the audience clapped.

_____

_____

10. In a formal letter, what should the heading include?

_____

_____

11. What is the final part of a formal letter?

_____

_____

LESSONS 1-8
REVIEW EXERCISES

Activity One

Circle the word or words that tell how the action occurred. Then write whether it is an adverb or a how phrase.

1. The baseball player hit a homerun with a wooden bat.

2. The chameleon caught a moth with its long tongue.

3. The wooden canoe smoothly glided down the river.

4. The dancers practiced in perfect unison.

5. The sharks hungrily swam near the reef.

6. The children curiously examined the fallen beehive.

7. With much anticipation, the families awaited the returning ship.

8. Some scientists study animals by observing their habitat.

9. President Theodore Roosevelt boxed regularly.

10. The skater gracefully glided across the ice.

11. Dad carried his briefcase by the handle.

12. The bird cleaned the alligator's teeth with its beak.

13. My sister learned painting techniques by attending art classes.

14. The detective cleverly solved the case.

Activity Two

Listed below are several basic sentences. In each sentence, add a subject describer phrase or word to tell exactly which subject the sentence is about.

EXAMPLE: The shoe is in the tree.

The shoe with the rainbow shoestrings is in the tree.

or

Those shoes are in the tree.

1. The gift is beautifully wrapped.

_____
_____

2. The bakery makes the best cinnamon rolls.

_____
_____

3. The boy won the race.

_____
_____

4. The president visited our country.

_____
_____

5. The keys belong to me.

_____
_____

6. People enjoy horseback riding, barbecues, and rodeos.

_____
_____

7. The fisherman went home.

8. Surfers catch awesome waves.

9. The car needs gas.

10. Islands offer warm, sandy beaches.

11. Architectural wonders are centuries old.

12. The pyramids are an unsolved mystery.

13. The firefighter rescued the family.

Activity Three

Re-write each sentence with an interjection. Look in Lesson Five for a list of interjections

EXAMPLE: I am surprised to see you.
   Wow! I am surprised to see you.

1. Your dog bit me.

_____

_____

2. We are the first to arrive.

_____

_____

3. I found your keys.

_____

_____

4. That sunset is beautiful.

_____

_____

5. I am exhausted.

_____

_____

6. Those fireworks were spectacular.

_____

_____

7. John received your letter.

_____

_____

8. I cannot go to the movies.

_____

_____

9. Are you ready?

_____

_____

10. Your cookies are delicious.

_____

_____

11. That painting is amazing.

_____

_____

12. I do not have any homework.

_____

_____

13. That was a hard workout.

_____

_____

14. I bit my tongue.

_____

_____

Activity Four

In items 1-7 use each simile in a complete sentence. In items 8-15 complete each sentence with a simile.

EXAMPLE: like thunder

The train sounded like thunder as it rolled through the town.

It rained like...

It rained like someone poured a bucket of water over my house.

1. big as a house

   _____

   _____

2. like a bird soaring through the air

   _____

   _____

3. black as night

   _____

   _____

4. as bright as day

   _____

   _____

5. like a fish in the water

   _____

   _____

6. clean as a whistle

7. hard as a nail

8. The boat rocked like

9. Like   , the children danced on the lawn.

10. The car sputtered like

11. I sat in my chair like

12. The dogs howled like

13. After Mount St. Helens erupted, the forest was flattened like a

Activity Five

Listed below are subjects/objects to be used in sentences. Create an appositive to accompany the subject/object and then write a complete sentence using the subject/object and the appositive.

EXAMPLE: Mrs. Ito

      Mrs. Ito, my neighbor, makes excellent fried rice.

1. the Mississippi

   _____

   _____

2. Beethoven

   _____

   _____

3. my kitten

   _____

   _____

4. the Eiffel Tower

   _____

   _____

5. Amy

   _____

   _____

6. our house

   _____

   _____

7. my computer

8. Washington D.C.

9. Dr. Seuss

10. the play

11. Mr. Parker

12. the panda bear

13. the movie

14. the Titanic

Activity Six

Listed below are two sets of subjects, verbs and objects. Create a complete sentence for each set and then combine the sentences with a prepositional phrase or a subject describer phrase. Add adjectives and adverbs to make the subjects and verbs interesting.

EXAMPLE: (boy, swam, river) (boy, swung, rope)

    The boy swam in the river. The boy swung on the rope.

    After the boy swung on the rope he swam in the river.

1. (athlete, competed, Olympics) (athlete, won, medal)

___

2. (Jamal, traveled, Europe) (Jamal, learned, languages)

___

3. (Frank, went, store) (Frank, bought, flowers)

___

4. (dolphin, jumped over, rope) (crowd, applauded)

___

5. (Earth, orbits, sun) (it, spins, top)

___

6. (Ulysses S. Grant, was, Civil War Hero)(he, was, eighteenth president)

7. (Babe Ruth, played, New York Yankees) (he, hit, sixty home runs in 1927)

8. (Renaissance, began, Rome) (scholars, studied, arts)

9. (I, read, book) (Pete, saw, movie)

Activity Seven

Diagram the following sentences using the diagram key in the reference section.

1. After the storm, we surveyed the damage.

2. The runners completed the race without stopping.

3. My family is going to Denmark on Sunday.

4. With courage and determination, the team maneuvered the raft through the rapids.

5. Franklin D. Roosevelt was the first president to appear on television.

6. The blue bird collected twigs for its nest.

7. Animals migrate to find better living conditions.

8. I accepted the award with pride.

9. Propellers thrust an airplane forward.

10. Mexico City is the capital of Mexico.

11. The Sahara is a desert in North Africa.

12. During the Industrial Revolution, city populations grew as workers searched for jobs.

LESSONS 9-12
REVIEW EXERCISES

Activity One

Complete the brainstorming clusters for the following topics. As you brainstorm details for the topics think about answering the questions: who, what, where, how, when, and why.

1. basketball

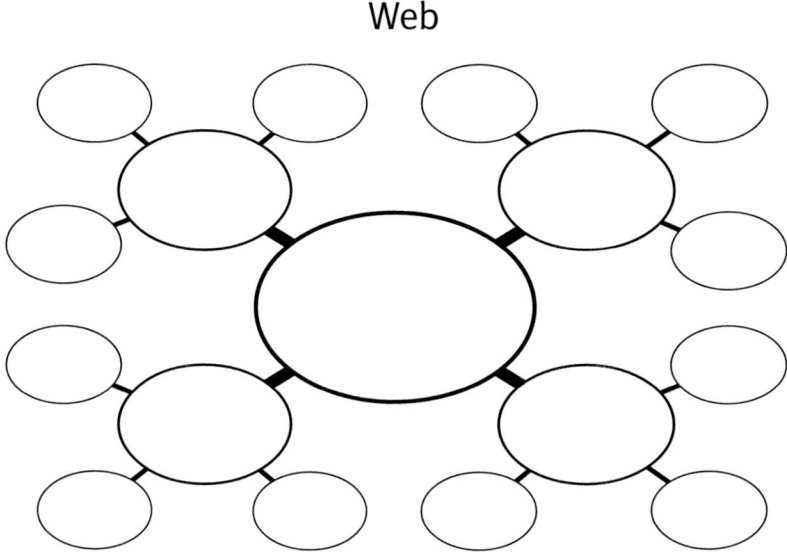

2. water safety

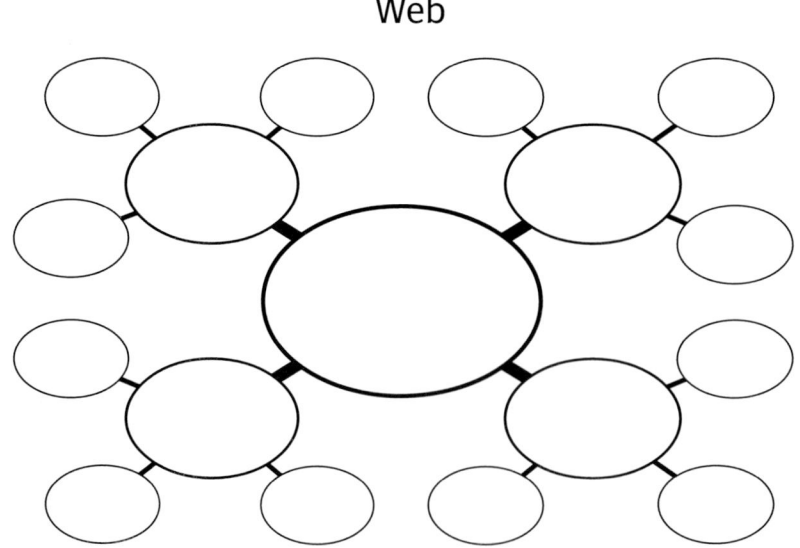

3. chores

Web

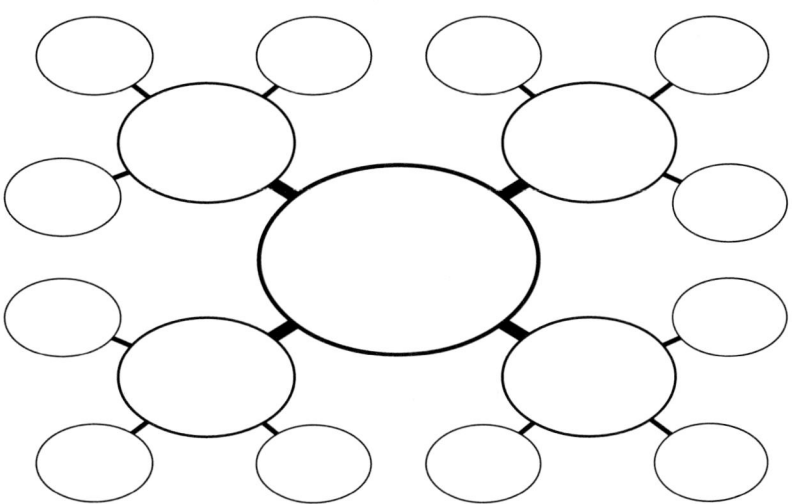

4. summer camp

Web

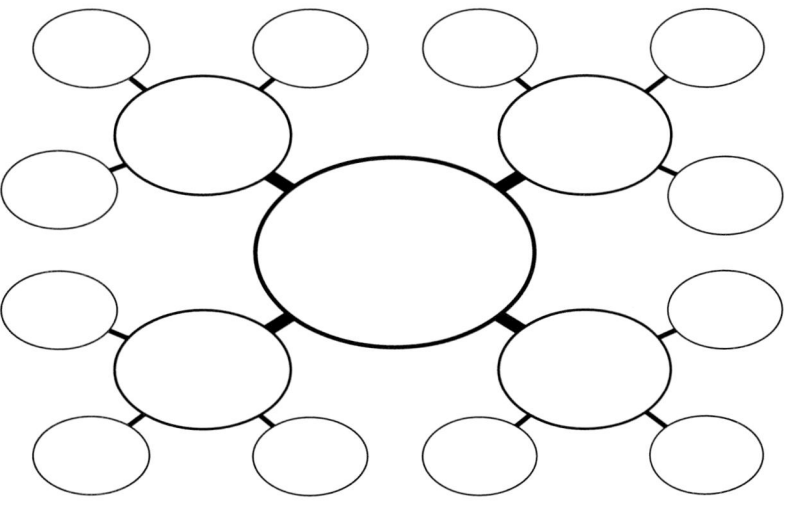

5. zoos/animal parks

Web

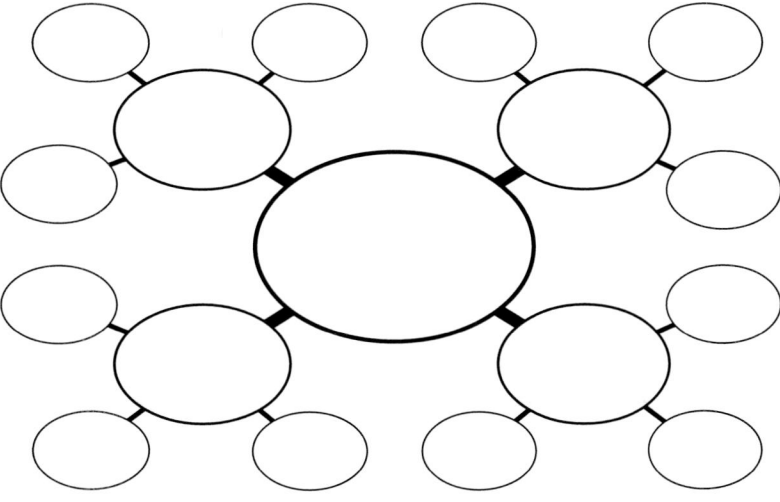

Activity Two

Use the brainstorming clusters you created in Activity One and write a topic sentence for each cluster.

1. _____

2. _____

3. _____

4. _____

5. _____

Activity Three

Edit the following informative paragraph. Look for capitalization, grammar, and punctuation errors.

are you looking for a fun, family vacation? Try camping. families can camp in many different locations Many beaches and lakes offer campsites near the water? also, the mountains and deserts have have parks designated for camping. When camping families enjoy outdoor activities such as hiking and fishing   in the evenings, families join around campfires to tell stories and sing songs! camping is great way to spend time with your family and enjoy nature

Activity Four

List three audiences who would be interested in the paragraph on camping.

1. _____

2. _____

3. _____

Activity Five

Listed below are three subjects/processes. Put the sentences in chronological order by numbering them from one to five.

1. Subject: baking cookies
   _____drop a spoonful of dough on the cookie sheet
   _____preheat the oven to 375 degrees
   _____mix flour, sugar, eggs, vanilla, and salt in a large bowl
   _____place the cookies on a rack to cool
   _____add chocolate chips to the mixture

2. Subject: washing a car
   _____rinse off the soapy water with the hose
   _____turn off the water and put away the hose
   _____fill a bucket with water and soap
   _____spray the car with water to get it wet
   _____use a sponge or a towel to clean the car with the soapy water

3. Subject: rock climbing
   _____hold onto the rope and slowly walk down the wall
   _____secure the safety harness around your waste
   _____climb up the rock wall by moving from rock to rock
   _____secure the rope to your harness and your partner's harness
   _____ring the bell when you reach the top

Activity Six

Now select one of the subjects from activity five and combine the sentences to create a chronological paragraph. Use the transition words *first, next, then, after that,* and *finally.* Elaborate on the details if you wish and include a topic sentence and conclusion.

LESSONS 13-17
REVIEW EXERCISES

Activity One

Diagram the following sentences using the diagram key in the reference section of your book.

1. I eat peanut butter and jelly sandwiches for lunch.

2. Tomorrow, the ship will set sail.

3. The tree branch eerily scratched the bedroom window during the storm.

4. The Apollo 11 lunar module landed on the moon in 1969.

5. Mrs. Garcia poured the butter over the popcorn.

6. The Amazon Rain Forest, found in South America, is home to many species of fascinating insects and beautiful animals.

7. The Spanish explorer Hernando Cortez landed on the shores of Mexico in 1519.

8. The horse bolted out of the gates with great speed.

9. Charles Dickens, an English author, wrote the classic story *A Christmas Carol*.

10. Wyatt's chores on the farm include feeding the livestock, cleaning the stalls, and milking the cows.

11. The long, colorful Chinese dragon paraded majestically down the crowded streets.

12. After Mom purchased the picnic supplies, she left without her change.

13. The space shuttle rocketed towards space after sunrise.

14. As rush hour traffic merged onto the freeway, our car moved as slow as molasses.

15. The white, frisky poodle jumped into the pool to fetch the ball.

Activity Two

The following paragraphs are written from the first person point of view. Re-write them in the third person.

1. I enjoy collecting stickers as a hobby. I visit stores in my neighborhood and look for unique, colorful stickers. My family always gives me stickers for my birthday and for holidays. I have a binder with pages for storing the stickers so they don't get lost. Sometimes my friends and I trade our stickers. I know I'll enjoy sticker collecting for a long time.

2. I think everyone should join a gym to stay fit. At the gym, I can use their equipment and request assistance from the trainers who teach proper form and technique. I enjoy the many exercising options at the gym. I can ride a stationary bike, swim in the pool, or take an aerobics or yoga class. Some people may complain that gyms are expensive, but I go regularly so it is worth the cost. Joe Smith, owner of Fit World told me, "The gym is a safe, comfortable place to get in shape and learn about staying fit. It is worth the investment." So join a gym today to stay strong and healthy.

Activity Three

Brainstorm the information for the following operational paragraphs.

1. **Purpose:** checking out a library book

   reader needs to know   **materials**   **steps**

2. **Purpose:** planting a seed

   reader needs to know   **materials**   **steps**

3. **Purpose:** building a fort

reader needs to know   materials   steps

4. **Purpose:** flying a kite

reader needs to know   materials   steps

Activity Four

Select one of your brainstorm topics from activity three and use the information to complete the outline below.

Topic Sentence/Main Idea
_____
_____

What you need
_____
_____

Step One   (first)
_____
_____

Step Two   (second, then)
_____
_____

Step Three   (third, next)
_____
_____

| Step Four | (fourth, after that) |

| Final Step | (last, finally) |

| Conclusion | |

Activity Five

Using your outline from activity four, write a rough draft using complete sentences and the transition words provided. Use a separate sheet of lined paper.

Activity Six

Now edit your rough draft and write the final draft for your operational paragraph on a separate sheet of lined paper.

LESSONS 18-23
REVIEW EXERCISES

Activity One

Fix the run-on sentences using punctuation or the connector words *and, or, because, so* or *as.*

1. The boys caught frogs in the pond built a bike ramp went skateboarding.

2. My class went to the zoo we saw polar bears hippos and koala bears.

3. The alarm sounded and the fire fighters put on their gear and jumped into the fire engines and sped to the scene of the fire.

4. During the storm the ship rocked in the waves the crew hid safely inside the hull.

5. I have six dollars the toy costs eight dollars.

6. For my birthday I received presents I had a party at the pizza place I played with my friends.

___

7. At the pool I jumped off of the diving board I swam in the deep end.

___

8. The fireworks exploded in the sky the colors were beautiful there were red, green, blue and gold lights.

___

9. The concert ended the audience applauded.

___

Activity Two

Following are two formal letters. Fill in the missing information to complete the formal letters.

1.

Joe Horsecamp
1234 Saddle Road
Horseville, MT 01234

Thank you for guiding the wonderful tour of your ranch. Our families learned about caring for horses, how to saddle and ride a horse, and about life on a ranch. We enjoyed your hospitality and look forward to our next visit.

Anna Gomer

2.

August 10, 2002

Sally Tennis
2020 Love Way
Tennisville, TX   01234

Please send information regarding your summer tennis camp. I would like to know the dates of your camp, the schedule, and the fees.

You can send the information to Charles Mendez, 1234 Sky Terrace, Cityville, TX 01123.

Thank you for your time.

Sincerely,

Activity Three

Read the following opening lines and decide which stylistic opener is being used: *a startling fact, a funny sound or story, a question, a confession, a famous quotation, dialogue,* or a *flashback.*

1. "There is no place like home." These are the famous final words spoken by Dorothy in *The Wizard of Oz.*

2. How did plants and animals get their names?

3. The sinking of the Titanic occurred in the cold, deep waters of the Atlantic Ocean.

4. Spitter, spatter, aughh, aughh, blahhh!

5. I have to admit, I did not spend enough time preparing for the test.

6. "Today is the big day," said my best friend Sam, "Are you ready?"

7. I remember the first day I took my new surfboard in the water and how I never thought I would learn to stand on the board in the waves.

8. Where did the summer go?

9. If I had not tried to be a show off with my bike, I would never have broken my arm.

10. The fifty foot tidal wave crashed into the village at noon, leveling the buildings and sweeping cars out into the ocean.

Activity Four

Use the diagram below to brainstorm similarities and differences for the listed topics.

1. summer and winter

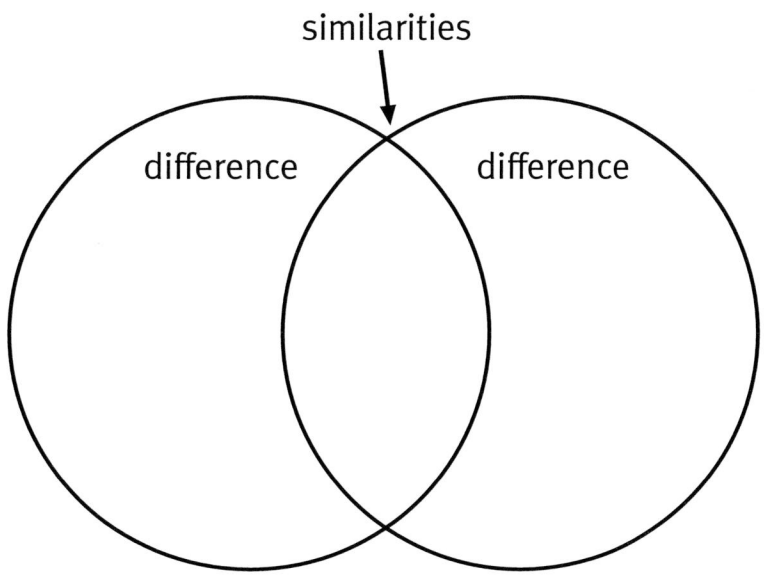

2. traveling by train and traveling by airplane

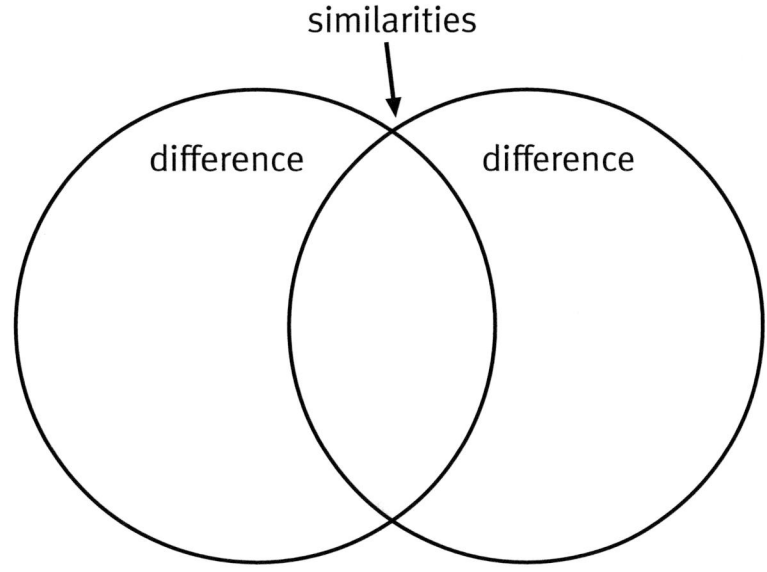

3. reading a book and watching a movie

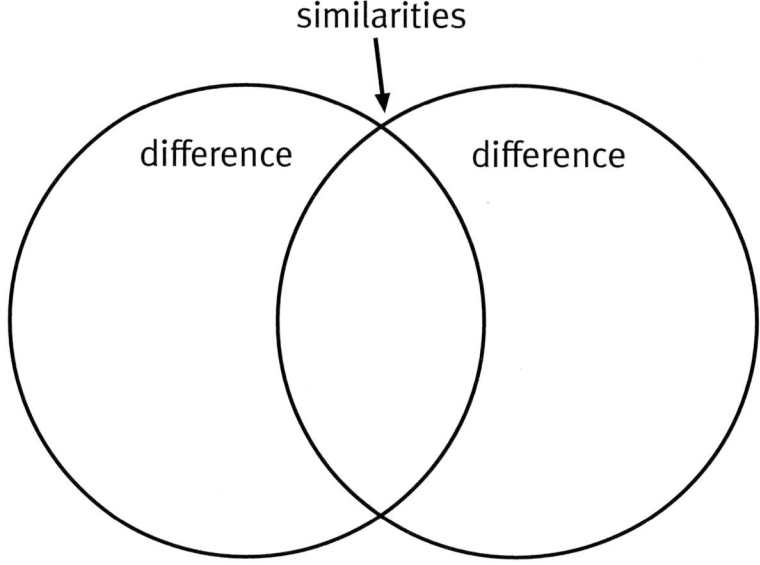

4. swimming at the beach and swimming in the pool

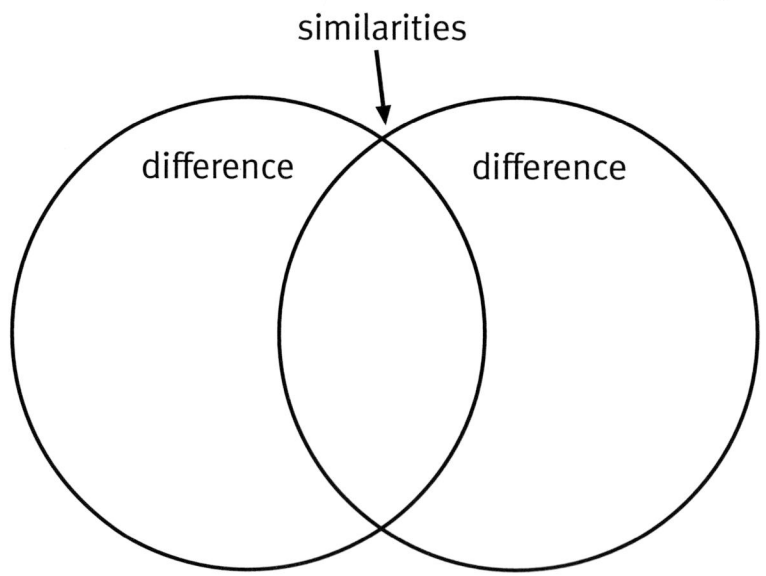

Activity Five

Think of as many sensory details as you can for the following subjects. List the details next to each sense.

1. ice cream

sight: _____

smell: _____

touch: _____

hearing: _____

taste: _____

2. forest

sight: _____

smell: _____

touch: _____

hearing: _____

taste: _____

3. fire

sight: _____

smell: _____

touch: _____

hearing: _____

taste: _____

4. bicycle:

sight: _____

smell: _____

touch: _____

hearing: _____

taste: _____

ANSWER KEY

Lesson One: Activity One

1. The autumn leaves glistened (in full color.) —phrase
2. The students (diligently) studied. —adverb
3. The little boy blinked (nervously.) —adverb
4. A snake sniffs (with its tongue.) —phrase
5. Jane crossed the quiet street (without caution.) —phrase
6. The snow storm struck (suddenly.) —adverb
7. (Without a care in the world,) Lisa napped in her hammock. —phrase
8. (With tears in her eyes,) Rachel confessed that she teased her brother. —phrase
9. (In a crashing boom,) the thunder exploded. —phrase
10. (Quickly,) he shut the book and turned out the light. —adverb
11. Rick finished his homework (with haste.) —phrase
12. The two candidates (nervously) shook hands. —adverb
13. (Instantly,) the phantom vanished. —adverb

Lesson One: Activity Two

1.   S V   O   when
   We will have a spelling test [on Friday.]
2.   AV   S V   O
   Tomorrow, we will visit the zoo.
3.   S   V   how
   The orchestra played in [harmony.]
4. S V   O   where
   Dad put the car keys in [his pocket.]
5.   how   S   V
   [With hope for the future,] President Lincoln signed the
     O
   Emancipation Proclamation.
6.   S   V   AV   AV
   Martin Luther King Jr. worked diligently and peacefully.
7.   S   V   O   how
   George Washington crossed the Delaware River [without fear.]
8. S V   where   when
   I am going [to Paris] [on Thursday.]
9.   S   AV   V   O   where
   The lion tamer courageously placed his head [inside the lion's mouth.]
10.   S   V   when
    The old fisherman fishes [in the morning.]
11.   how   S V   O
    [With heavy eyelids,] the little girl kissed her parents goodnight.
12.   S   AV   V   where
    The gazelle gracefully ran [across the savanna.]
13.   S   V   where   how
    Anne Frank wrote [in her diary] [with dedication.]
14.   AV   S   V   O   O   O
    Triumphantly, Helen Keller learned reading, writing, and arithmetic.
15.   S   V   AV
    The clock chimed melodically.

Lesson Two: Activity One

1. Some people say that frog legs taste (like chicken.) —simile
2. (Like booming thunder,) the audience clapped. —simile
3. The oak tree swayed (wildly) in the wind. —adverb
4. The heavy rain fell (like a gushing waterfall.) —simile
5. The stray dog walked (with a limp.) —phrase
6. The eagle soared (with grace.) —phrase
7. The glass fell (without breaking.) —phrase
8. The helicopter hovered above the building (like a bee above a flower.) —simile
9. My dog jumped (like a grasshopper.) —simile
10. The children listened (with eagerness.) —phrase
11. My voice sounded (like a frog croaking.) —simile
12. (Like a pro,) he hit the hockey puck into the goal. —simile
13. (With great care,) John folded his clothes. —phrase
14. He told his joke (without laughing.) —phrase
15. One day, cars will fly (like airplanes.) —simile

Lesson Two: Activity Three

1.   S V AV   when
   The snow fell heavily [on Christmas Eve night.]
2.   S   V   AV   when
   The bear growled ferociously [while protecting her young.]

3. My mom goes [to bed] early [every night].
   S V where AV when

4. [During rush hour,] the cars move [like turtles].
   when S V simile

5. The lightning flashed suddenly [in the distance].
   S V AV where

6. [In the corners of the basement,] the spiders spin their webs.
   where S V O

7. [During the Civil War,] Harriet Tubman saved many lives
   when S V O
   [with the Underground Railroad.]
   how

8. My ring fell [between the rocks] [during our hike].
   S V where when

9. [On Valentine's Day,] Emily signed the letter [with love].
   when S V O how

10. [Without warning,] the cold winter descended [upon us].
    how S V where

11. [Against her mother's advice,] she rode her bike [without a helmet].
    how S V O how

12. [During the ninth inning,] the team pulled together and
    when S V AV
    won the game.
    V O

13. [During the afternoon,] the black street is [as hot as a frying pan].
    when S V simile

14. [After the game,] the large crowd moved quickly [like a stampede].
    when S V AV simile

15. [Like a kaleidoscope,] our large garden is filled [with beautiful, bright flowers.]
    simile S V C how

Lesson Three: Activity One

1. The children ran through the sprinklers (because they were hot.)
2. The snake rests under the bush (to cool its body.)
3. Mom cut up the hot dog (for the baby.)
4. The class boarded the bus (for the field trip.)
5. Dad went to the sale (so he could save money.)
6. The polar bear dove in the water (to get the fish.)
7. (Because he was too small,) my little brother could not go on the roller coaster.
8. Elizabeth Cady Stanton worked hard (for women's rights.)
9. Eleanor Roosevelt created programs (to help the poor.)
10. (To preserve our natural resources,) Theodore Roosevelt created the National Parks system.
11. Mom went to the store (to get some milk.)
12. Jake tied his shoes (so he wouldn't trip and fall.)
13. We visit the Wildlife Refuge (to learn about endangered species.)
14. (Because he was tired and hungry,) the baby cried loudly.
15. She asked me (for help.)

Lesson Three: Activity Two

1. The cat sat [on the floor] [to clean her paws.]
   S V where why

2. [In Antarctica,] penguins fish [in cold waters.]
   where S V where

3. [Like humans,] chimpanzees are primates.
   simile S V C

4. Dolphins use echolocation [to communicate and find their way.]
   S V O why

5. The Bill of Rights was written [to insure our individual freedoms.]
   S V C why

6. Gallileo studied constellations [so he could better understand the universe.]
   S V O why

7. [In 1492,] Christopher Columbus set sail [to discover a new route to Asia.]
   when S V O why

8. [During the 16th century,] Queen Elizabeth I was a very powerful leader.
   when S V AV C

9. [In China,] pandas are protected [because they are an endangered species.]
   where S V C why

10. Coral reefs can be found [in warm, shallow waters.]
    S V C where

11. A chameleon changes color [to protect itself from predators.]
    S V O why

12. My mother planted tulip bulbs [before spring.]
    S V O when

13. [Because it was over hunted,] the American Buffalo became nearly extinct.
    why S V AV C

14. We use our lungs [to breathe.]
    S V O why

15. Daniel Boone was a famous frontiersman.
    S V C

Lesson Four: Activity One

1. The sand dunes (in Morro Bay) move a few inches each year.
2. The little girl (with the green hat) is a girl scout.
3. The rings (of Saturn) are made up of ice, rock, and dust.
4. The cable cars (of San Francisco) are a familiar sight.
5. The girl (on the horse) is wearing a helmet.
6. People (in Japan) eat a lot of fish and rice.
7. The signers (of the Declaration of Independence) were notable men.
8. The president (of the United States) is a powerful person.
9. (That) mouse stole the cheese.
10. (Those) windmills generate electricity.
11. The racoon (with the large tail) rummaged through the trash.
12. (These) books are for the children.
13. The sign (on the door) is a warning.

Lesson Four: Activity Two

1. S   V C
   The shells |along the shore| are broken.
2. S V O where
   We get milk [from cows.]
3. where   S   V   C
   [In legends,] mermaids were a sign |of disaster.|
4. S   V C O
   The cat |on the fence| is hunting mice.
5. S   V   where
   A newborn kangaroo stays [in its mother's pouch.]
6. S   V   O
   Pheidippides was the man |who ran with the news of Greek
   when
   victory| [after the Battle of Marathon.]
7. S V   C where
   Los Angeles is the second largest city [in the United States.]
8. S   V   C
   Female lions do most of the hunting.
9. S   V   O where
   Charles Lindbergh made a historic flight [across the
   Atlantic Ocean.]
10. S   V C
    The Statue of Liberty was a gift |from France.|
11. S   V   where   where
    The Mona Lisa hangs [in the Louvre Museum] [in Paris.]

12. when   S V   O
    [In autumn,] deciduous trees lose their leaves.
13. S   V   simile
    My brother's room looked [like a bomb hit it.]
14. S   V C where
    President John F. Kennedy was born [in Brookline, Massachusetts.]
15. S   V O
    The Mayan people |of Central America| grew corn and sweet
    O   where
    potatoes [on communal lands.]

Lesson Five: Activity One

1. ✓ Ouch! That hurt.
2. ✓ No, I don't have a dog.
3. ✓ Oh! That's my favorite flower.
4. ✓ Hey! Where were you last night?
5. ✓ Wow! Your new haircut looks great.
6. ✓ Yes, we will be leaving soon.
7. ✓ Phew! That was hard.
8. ✓ Goodness! You are a handful.
9. ✓ Well, should we go?
10. ✓ Gee whiz! It was just an accident.

Lesson Six: Activity One

1. (In my opinion,) bats are fascinating creatures.
2. John, (therefore,) decided to do the project.
3. (To tell the truth,) I'd rather see the other movie.
4. James, (however,) is not a good friend.
5. (In fact,) several people agree with the candidate.
6. (For example,) we could spend the day at the beach.
7. (I suppose,) the teacher can help you with your work.
8. (In the first place,) Chris doesn't have a bike.
9. She, (too,) received an A on the test.
10. (If you ask me,) he will make a good class president.

Lesson Six: Activity Three

1. (If you ask me,) that dog is not friendly.
   S V AV/C
   (with "that" boxed)

2. The deer hiding in the forest were still [until the hunters left.]
   S ___ V C when

3. [During the storm,] we played games and ate popcorn.
   when S V O V O

4. I found the green bike [in the river.]
   S V O where

5. Yikes! That water is cold.
   ✓ S V C

6. I placed the hot apple pie [on the table.]
   S V O where

7. Those dolphins enjoy riding the waves [on the beaches of Florida.]
   S V O where

8. The captain of the ship ordered the crew [to man the battle stations.]
   S V O why

9. The young writer nervously accepted the Pulitzer Prize.
   S AV V O

10. Sophia, (too,) enjoys horseback riding [on the trail.]
    S V O where

11. Sean, (however,) went in [without a wet suit.]
    S V how

12. (To tell the truth,) I like the red one best.
    S V O AV

Lesson Seven: Activity One

1. Kabuki, (a form of theatre,) is very popular in Japan.

2. In the musical (Oklahoma,) Curly and Judd are rivals.

3. Machu Pichu, (an ancient ruin in Peru,) is visited by many tourists.

4. My friend (Elizabeth) has that book.

5. Frances, (my younger sister,) is taller than I.

6. One of the longest streets in Boston, (Beacon Street,) is lined with trees.

7. Our clock, (an antique grandfather clock,) chimes on the hour.

8. Yesterday, I met Mrs. Green, (the new fourth grade teacher.)

9. Today, our class read from A Bridge to Terebithia, (my favorite book.)

10. The Statue of Liberty, (a famous American landmark,) greets immigrants from all over the world.

11. The Netherlands, (a country in Europe,) is famous for tulips and windmills.

12. The musical (Cats) was the longest running musical on Broadway.

13. We visited the Egyptian Pyramids, (one of the Seven Wonders of the World.)

Lesson Seven: Activity Two

1. Mice look for shelter [during the winter.]
   S V O when

2. Gee whiz! I was only kidding.
   ✓ S V AV C

3. That dog barks [like a squeaking mouse.]
   S V simile

4. Tea grown in China is the best [in the world.]
   S V C where

5. Ivan the Terrible was the first czar of Russia.
   S V C

6. Indiana's most famous annual event is the Indianapolis 500.
   AV S V C

7. My brother David takes martial arts lessons [after school.]
   S △ V O when

8. (In the first place,) I can't find the address.
   S V C O

9. The Ganges, a river in India, is sacred [to Hindus.]
   S △ V C how

10. [Because it is unpredictable,] a hurricane can cause a lot of damage.
    why S V C O

11. The giraffe is the tallest animal [in the world.]
    S V C where

12. (Once again,) the capital of Germany is now Berlin.
    S V AV C

13. The Hindu lawyer Mohandas Gandhi helped [to free India]
    S △ V why
    [through peaceful means.]
    how

Lesson Eight: Activity One

1. After dinner was cooked, we sat down at the table.

2. Juan, who is in fourth grade, finished his homework.

3. When the earthquake stopped rumbling, we went outside to look for damage.

4. During medieval times, serfs and lords lived on manors.

5. During its maiden voyage, the Titanic sank in the icy Atlantic Ocean.

6. Jamie went to the library and checked out a story book.

7. The Jamestown colonists, who were from England, settled on the James River.

8. Mr. Martinez bought a bike that he rides to the store.

9. The children cheered as the school bus arrived.
10. My grandfather, a carpenter, makes beautiful wooden toys.
11. When the photograher saw children playing in the fountain, he quickly began taking pictures.
12. The eastern seaboard has a thriving fishing industry of lobster, crab, and cod.

Lesson Eight: Activity Two

Jan, who lives on a farm, knows a lot about taking care of animals. After she gets up in the morning, Jan goes into the stable and cleans her horse's stall. She also feeds the horse and cleans its hooves. After that, Jan feeds the chickens pellets and gathers the eggs. Jan likes to take care of the animals, and the animals like Jan too.

The early Native American tribes were resourceful. They took from the earth and gave back to the earth. They planted crops, fished in rivers, and hunted deer and buffalo. The Indian tribes used the meat for food and the hides for clothing and shelter. The Indians also sang songs and danced to thank mother earth for providing these resources.

Cruise ships offer unique vacations that are luxurious and full of adventure. Ships have many activities such as swimming, shuffle board, and rock climbing. Kids can play games or do arts and crafts. Ships offer fabulous gourmet meals such as seafood, salads, and desserts. The cruise ships go to unique places such as Mexico, the Bahamas, and Alaska.

Cumulative Review Lessons 1-8

1. Johnny rode his bike with caution.
2. with, without, in
3. simile
4. Because she was frightened, Tina slept with the light on.
5. for, to, because
6. The shell with the ridges is the prettiest.
7. That horse has a long mane.
8. interjection
9. parenthetical expression
10. Diego Rivera, a Mexican artist, is well known for his murals.
11. prepositional phrases and subject describer phrases.
12. Go pick up the little boy who is crying.

Lesson Ten: Activity One

1.
   A. first graders
   B. an X should be on the words: sub-saharan, species, and agile.
   C. 5-7 minutes
   D. A star should be next to thefollowing:
      Why the cheetah is so fast
      What the cheetah looks like
      Shanta: The cheetah that saved a little girl's life

2. The following audiences should be circled:
      School-aged children
      Parents for Safety

3. Dolphins: Our friends from the ocean The damaging effects of sunburns.

Lesson 12: Activity One

The sentences should be numbered as follows:

2 The green car was in front of the yellow car.
5 The yellow car slammed on its brakes, but it was too late. He hit the green car.
1 I was walking my dog along the lake.
4 The man in the yellow car was talking on his phone.
3 The green car turned on its blinker and slowed.

Lesson 12: Activity two

3 The males have tusks which protrude from beneath the nose.
1 This animal has two large ears on the sides of its head.
5 This animal has four legs beneath its enormous gray body.
4 Its tail hangs from the top of its back to the middle of its legs.
2 It has a long nose which can move flexibly from left to right or up and down.

Elephant

2 Its right arm is extended upward holding a torch.
1 This American landmark is on the east coast.
5 Its feet stand upon a concrete foundation on an island.
3 A crown sits atop its head.
4 A gown hangs from her shoulder to the ground.

The Statue of Liberty

1. He was often found in the White House.
5. He wore black pants over his gangly legs.
4. Long thin arms hung next to his body.
3. He had a dark beard.
2. A tall black hat was often seen on his head.

Abraham Lincoln

Lesson 12: Activity Three

1. Most important
2. Least important
3. Most important

Lesson 15: Activity One

1. Third person
2. First person
3. Third person
4. Third person
5. First person
6. First person
7. Third person
8. First person
9. First person
10. First person
11. Third person
12. Third person
13. First person
14. Third person
15. First person

Lesson 15: Activity Two

When looking for a summer job, follow a few specific steps. First, look through a newspaper and find a job opening that interests you. Also, make sure that you have the skills required for the job. Second, contact the employer and request an appointment to fill out an application and be interviewed. When preparing for the interview, dress for success so you feel confident. Finally, arrive at the appointment on time and with all the information needed to complete the application. By following these steps, you are sure to find a fulfilling summer job.

Cumulative Review 13-17

1. operational
2. Purpose
   What reader needs to know
   materials
   steps
3. How and Why
4. I, me, my
5. third person
6. persuasive
7. reasons
8. facts
   expert
   opposition
   consequence

Lesson 18: Activity One

1. Question
2. Confession
3. Dialogue
4. Story
5. Quotation
6. Fact

Lesson 20: Activity Three

Graduation day was finally here. <u>The sun was warm and glowing over the spring lawn filled with families and friends.</u> [sensory] Looking back, it was a perfect day. <u>I can remember feeling nothing but pride for the hard work and perseverence I had dedicated to my studies during the past four years.</u> [memory] <u>In my hands the diploma felt crisp.</u> [sensory] As I spotted <u>my family</u> [reflective] in the boisterous crowd, I knew their support would always <u>follow me.</u> How lucky I felt to know that others believed in me as I believed in myself.

Lesson 22: Activity One

1. The school bell rang signaling the beginning of classes. The children ran indoors.
2. The holiday traffic was heavy. There were many small accidents on the road.
3. Mother went to the grocery store. She bought my favorite snack.
4. The lights dimmed, the audience grew quiet, and the orchestra began.
5. The tea kettle steamed and whistled. Ann turned off the stove and poured the water in the teapot.
6. The rain pounded on the roof. Gloria reached for her umbrella before leaving the house.
7. The plane pulled away from the gate. It taxied to the runway.
8. The audience stood. The president entered the room.
9. The children argued over the doll. Mother took the doll away.
10. The ice cream dripped from the cone. Josh licked the cone trying to get every bite.

Lesson 22: Activity Two

1. The school bell rang signaling the beginning of classes, so the children ran indoors.
2. The holiday traffic was heavy, because there were many small accidents on the road.
3. Mother went to the grocery store and bought my favorite snack.
4. The lights dimmed, the audience grew quiet, and the orchestra began.
5. The tea kettle steamed and whistled, so Ann turned off the stove and poured the water in the teapot.
6. The rain pounded on the roof, so Gloria reached for her umbrella before leaving the house.
7. The plane pulled away from the gate and taxied to the runway.
8. The audience stood as the president entered the room.
9. The children argued over the doll, so Mother took the doll away.
10. The ice cream dripped from the cone, as Josh licked the cone trying to get every bite.

Lesson 22: Activity Three

A warm summer day at a professional baseball game is good family fun. It is exciting to watch the pitchers throw the ball from the mound. When the batters swing, the crowd always anticipates contact and watches the ball to see if it sails into the stands. It is a good idea to bring a mitt in case you are lucky enough to catch a foul ball or a homer. Sometimes the batter will sign the ball for you after the game. The concessions stands usually offer excellent hot dogs, fries, and ice cream. Souvenirs such as baseball hats and T-shirts can also be purchased. Whether your favorite team wins or loses, you still have a great time.

During the 1906 San Francisco Earthquake, my grandmother saved a handful of gold. At 8:56 am my grandmother's house on Fell Street began to shake. Quickly the tremors increased and things began to fall from the ceiling and the walls. Without thinking my grandmother and her 12 brothers and sisters ran from the house. They looked back to see the roof catch fire. When the earthquake and aftershocks ended and the fire was put out, nothing remained but ashes. As my grandmother sifted through the rubble looking for mementos, she uncovered a handful of Chilean gold coins, all that was left of her family's fortune.

Cumulative Review 18-23

1. Startling fact
2. Quotation
3. Similarities
4. Differences
5. Sensory
6. Memory
7. Reflective
8. Run-on
9. The pianist played the final note and the audience clapped.
10. date, your name and address, the name and address of the person you are writing to.
11. Closing and signature

Topics

Area of Expertise

Write about a subject such as a craft, hobby, or sport that you have a good deal of experience with.
1. **Inform** your audience of the important aspects of your topic.
2. Write an **operational** paragraph/essay explaining the process of your subject.
3. **Persuade** your audience that you are an expert in your subject
4. **Compare** or **contrast** your subject with another.

Memorable Firsts

Write about a memorable first experience such as your first day of school.
1. **Inform** your audience of the important aspects of your topic.
2. **Compare** or **contrast** your subject with another.

School Memories

Write about a memorable school experience such as winning an award.
1. **Inform** your audience of the important aspects of your topic.
2. **Compare** or **contrast** your subject with another.

Unforgettable People

Write about a person you have met that made an unforgettable impact on your life.
1. **Inform** your audience of the important aspects of your topic.
2. **Compare** or **contrast** your the person with another person.

Unforgettable Places

Write about a place you have been that made an unforgettable impact on your life.
1. **Inform** your audience of the important aspects of your topic.
2. **Persuade** your audience to visit this place.
3. **Compare** or **contrast** this place with another place.

Favorites

Write about your favorite food, toy, sport, hobby, restaurant, etc.
1. **Inform** your audience of the important aspects of your topic.
2. Write an **operational** paragraph/essay explain how to enjoy your topic.
3. **Persuade** your audience to make your topic their favorite too.
4. **Compare** or **contrast** your topic with another.

Things to Change

Write about something you think should change such as the school dress code.
1. **Inform** your audience of the important aspects of your topic.
2. Write an **operational** paragraph/essay explaining how to make the necessary changes.
3. **Persuade** your audience to agree that it shouldbe changed.
4. **Compare** or **contrast** your topic with something else that should or should not change.

Pet Peeve

Write about your biggest pet peeve.
1. **Inform** your audience of the important aspects of your topic.
2. **Persuade** your audience to eliminate this peeve.
3. **Compare** or **contrast** your pet peeve with something that does or does not bother you.

The Environment

Choose an environmental topic such as recycling to discuss in your paragraph or essay.
1. **Inform** your audience of the important aspects of your topic.
2. Write an **operational** paragraph/essay such as how to recycle.
3. **Persuade** your audience to agree or disagree about recycling.
4. **Compare** or **contrast** your topic with another environmental topic.

School Violence

Write about violence in your school or your country.
1. **Inform** your audience of the important aspects of school violence.
2. Write an **operational** paragraph/essay on how to reduce school violence.
3. **Persuade** your audience to get active about stopping school violence
4. **Compare** or **contrast** school violence with violence nation wide.

Learning a Foreign Language

Think about your experiences learning another language when writing on one of the following topics.

1. **Inform** your audience of the requirements your school district has for learning a foreign language.
2. Write an **operational** paragraph/essay on the best way to learn a foreign language.
3. **Persuade** your audience of the benefits of learning another language.
4. **Compare** or **contrast** learning a foreign language with learning your native language.

Music

1. **Inform** your audience about your favorite music singer or group.
2. Write an **operational** paragraph/essay on playing a certain instrument.
3. **Persuade** your audience to listen to a certain type of music.
4. **Compare** or **contrast** your favorite type of music with another type of music.

Movie Ratings

1. **Inform** your audience of the important aspects of movie ratings.
2. **Persuade** your audience to change the current movie rating system.
3. **Compare** or **contrast** G-rated movies with PG-rated movies.

School Uniforms

1. **Inform** your audience of the current uniforms or dress code at your school.
2. **Persuade** your audience to change the current uniform or dress code system.
3. **Compare** or **contrast** your uniforms or dress code with the dress code at your parent's place of employment.

Homework

1. **Inform** your audience of the current homework requirements at your school
2. **Persuade** your audience to change the current homework requirements.
3. **Compare** or **contrast** your homework requirements with those at another school.

Mandatory Testing

1. **Inform** your audience of any mandatory testing required at your school or by your state.
2. Write an **operational** paragraph/essay on how best to prepare for mandatory tests.
3. **Persuade** your audience to change the current mandatory testing.
4. **Compare** or **contrast** mandatory testing with the current grading system in your school.

Drug Prevention

1. **Inform** your audience of any existing drug prevention program in your school or community.
2. Write an **operational** paragraph/essay on how to keep children away from drugs.
3. **Persuade** your audience to become involved in a drug prevention program.

Volunteering

1. **Inform** your audience of any volunteer activities you participate in.
2. Write an **operational** paragraph/essay on how to become a volunteer.
3. **Persuade** your audience to volunteer in the community.
4. **Compare** or **contrast** your volunteer activities with those of other people you may know.

Web

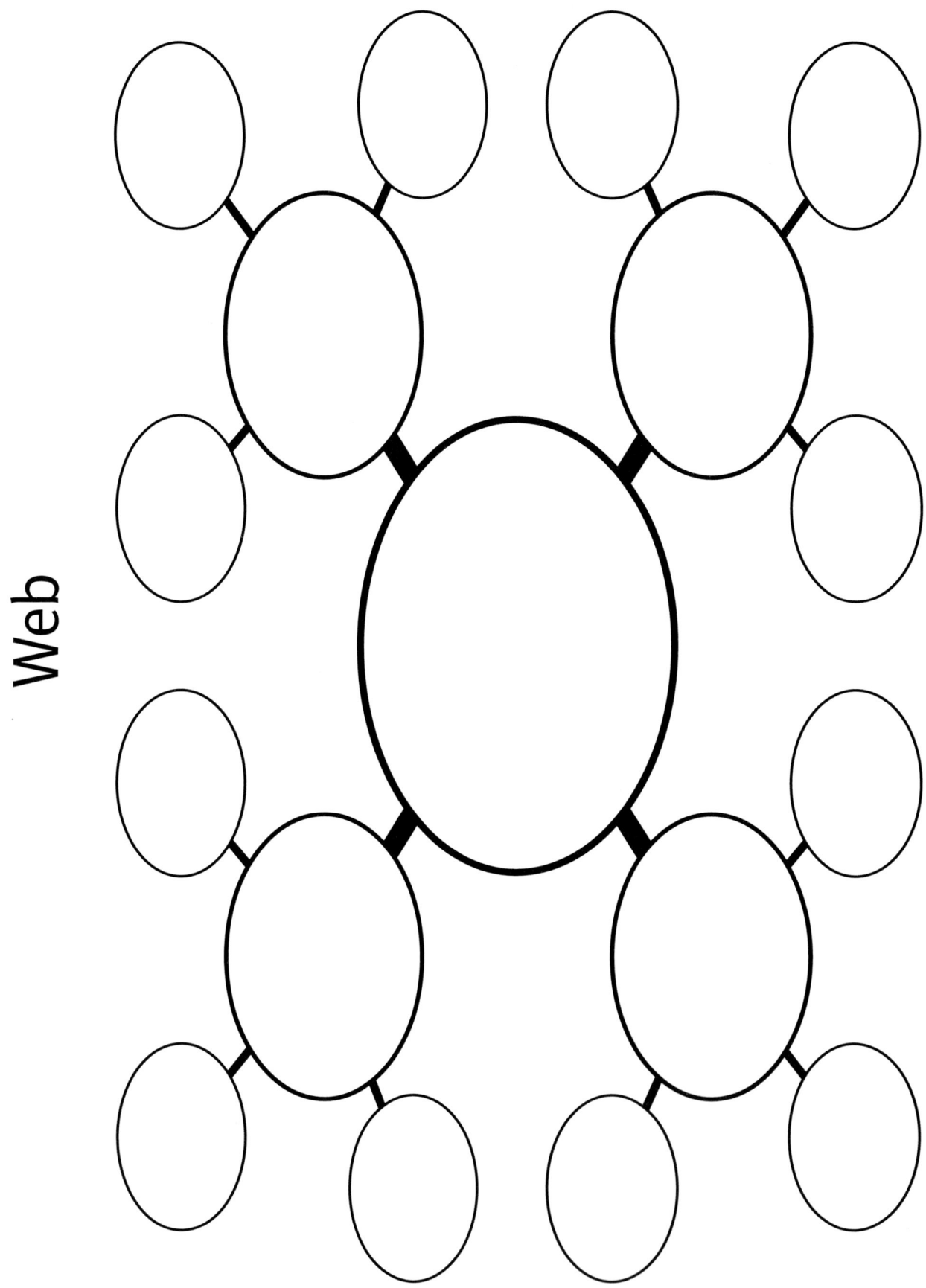

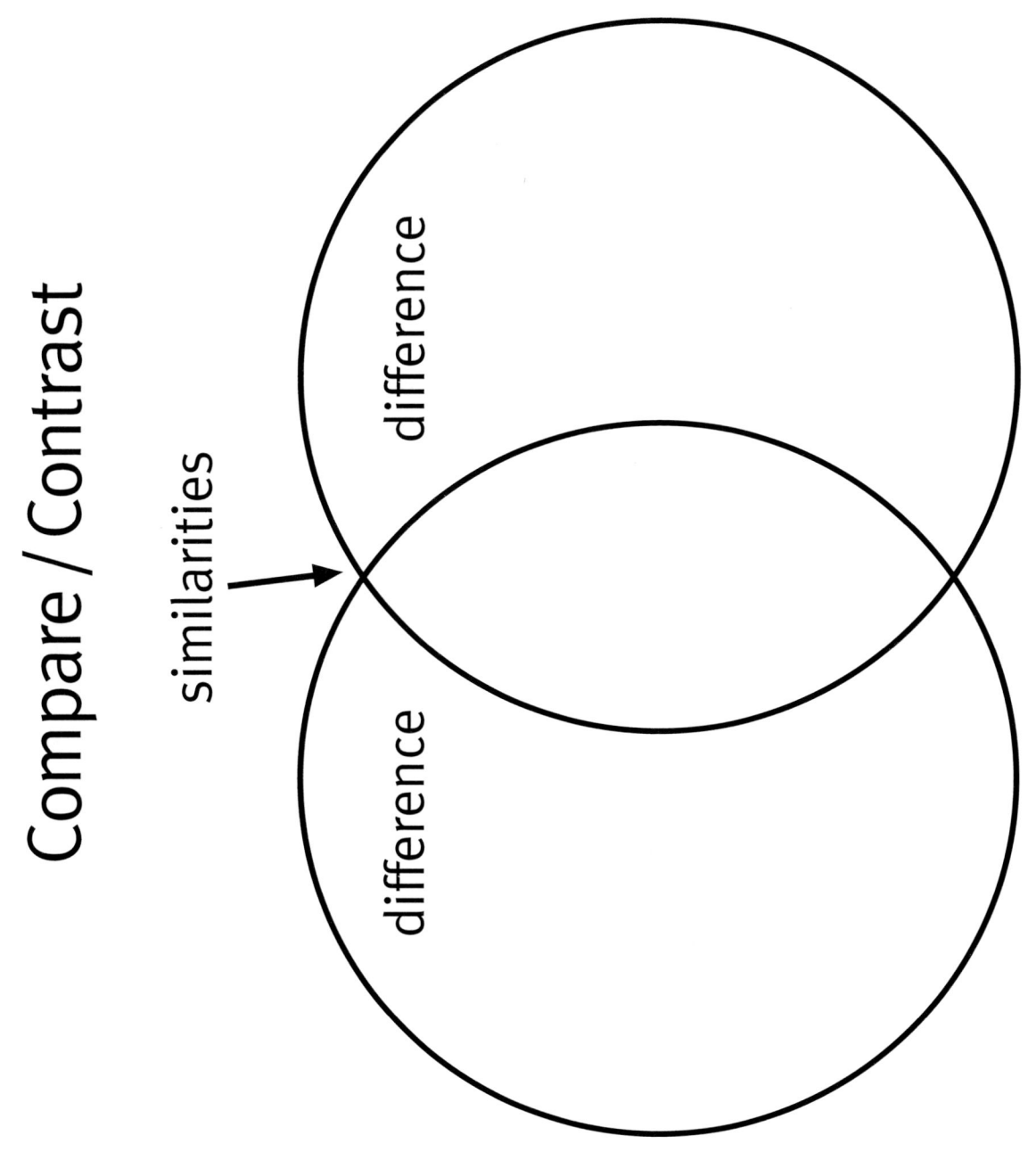

Informative Paragraph

Topic Sentence/Main Idea

Detail Sentence (first, one)

Detail Sentence (second, next, also)

Detail Sentence (third, after that, as well)

Detail Sentence (last, finally)

Conclusion Sentence

Informative Essay

Introductory Paragraph

Topic Sentence: _____

_____

_____

What Will Reader Learn: _____

_____

_____

Why Does Reader Want to Know: _____

_____

_____

Detail Paragraph 1   (first, one)

Topic Sentence: _____

_____

_____

Detail: _____

Detail: _____

Detail: _____

Example: _____

Transitional Sentence: _____

_____

Informative Essay

Detail Paragraph 2   (second, next, another)

Topic Sentence: _____

_____

_____

Detail: _____

Detail: _____

Detail: _____

Example: _____

Transitional Sentence: _____

_____

Detail Paragraph 3   (third, also, in addition)

Topic Sentence: _____

_____

_____

Detail: _____

Detail: _____

Detail: _____

Example: _____

Transitional Sentence: _____

_____

Informative Essay

Last Detail Paragraph   (last, finally)

Topic Sentence: _____

_____

_____

Detail: _____

Detail: _____

Detail: _____

Example: _____

Transitional Sentence: _____

_____

Final Paragraph

Conclusion/Clincher: _____

_____

_____

Personal Thought: _____

_____

_____

Call to Action: _____

_____

_____

Operational Paragraph

Topic Sentence/Main Idea

_____

_____

What you need

_____

_____

Step One (first)

_____

_____

Step Two (second, then)

_____

_____

Step Three (third, next)

_____

_____

Operational Paragraph

Step Four   (fourth, after that)
_____
_____
_____

Final Step   (last, finally)
_____
_____
_____

Conclusion
_____
_____
_____

Operational Essay

Introductory Paragraph

Topic Sentence: _____
_____
_____

Why: _____
_____

What You Need: _____
_____
_____

Transitional Sentence: _____
_____
_____

Step 1 Paragraph   (first)

Topic Sentence: _____
_____
_____

How: _____

Why: _____

Operational Essay

Step 2 Paragraph (second, then)

Topic Sentence: _____

_____

_____

How: _____

Why: _____

Step 3 Paragraph (third, next)

Topic Sentence: _____

_____

_____

How: _____

Why: _____

Last Step Paragraph (last, finally)

Topic Sentence: _____

_____

_____

How: _____

Why: _____

Operational Essay

Final Paragraph

Conclusion/Clincher: _____

_____

_____

Personal Thought: _____

_____

_____

Call to Action: _____

_____

_____

Persuasive Paragraph

Topic Sentence/Main Idea
___
___
___

Detail Sentence   (the first reason)
___
___
___

Detail Sentence   (another reason, secondly)
___
___
___

Detail Sentence   (as well, furthermore)
___
___
___

Detail Sentence   (last, finally)
___
___
___

Conclusion Sentence
___
___
___

Persuasive Essay

Introductory Paragraph

Topic Sentence: _____
_____
_____

Summarize the Details: _____
_____
_____

Transitional Sentence: _____
_____
_____

Paragraph 1 – Give the Facts

Topic Sentence: _____
_____
_____

Fact: _____

Fact: _____

Fact: _____

Transitional Sentence: _____
_____
_____

Persuasive Essay

Paragraph 2 – Refer to an Expert

Topic Sentence: _____

_____

_____

Quote from Expert: _____

_____

_____

Transitional Sentence: _____

_____

_____

Paragraph 3 – Answer the Opposition

Topic Sentence: _____

_____

_____

What the Opposition Says: _____

_____

Refute the Opposition: _____

_____

Transitional Sentence: _____

_____

_____

Persuasive Essay

Paragraph 4 – State Likely Consequences

Topic Sentence: _____

_____

_____

Consequence: _____

Consequence: _____

Consequence: _____

Transitional Sentence: _____

_____

_____

Final Paragraph

Conclusion/Clincher: _____

_____

_____

Personal Thought: _____

_____

_____

Call to Action: _____

_____

_____

Comparison Paragraph

Topic Sentence/Main Idea
_____
_____

Detail Sentence (one way)
_____
_____

Detail Sentence (also)
_____
_____

Detail Sentence (in addition)
_____
_____

Detail Sentence (last, finally)
_____
_____

Conclusion Sentence
_____
_____

Contrast Paragraph

Topic Sentence/Main Idea

_____
_____
_____

Detail Sentence (Subject One)   (first of all)

_____
_____
_____

Detail Sentence (Subject Two)   (on the other hand)

_____
_____
_____

Detail Sentence (Subject One)   (secondly)

_____
_____
_____

Detail Sentence (Subject Two)   (however)

_____
_____
_____

Detail Sentence (Subject One)   (finally)

_____
_____
_____

Contrast Paragraph

Detail Sentence (Subject Two)   (in contrast)
_____
_____

Conclusion Sentence
_____
_____

Comparison Essay

Introductory Paragraph

Topic Sentence: _____

_____

_____

Summarize the Details: _____

_____

_____

Why Does Reader Want to Know: _____

_____

_____

Detail Paragraph 1   (one way)

Topic Sentence: _____

_____

_____

Detail: _____

Elaborate: _____

_____

_____

Transitional Sentence: _____

_____

Comparison Essay

Detail Paragraph 2 (also, another way)

Topic Sentence: _____

_____

_____

Detail: _____

Elaborate: _____

_____

_____

Transitional Sentence: _____

_____

Detail Paragraph 3 (in addition)

Topic Sentence: _____

_____

_____

Detail: _____

Elaborate: _____

_____

_____

Transitional Sentence: _____

_____

Comparison Essay

Last Detail Paragraph   (last, finally)

Topic Sentence: _____
_____
_____

Detail: _____

Elaborate: _____
_____
_____

Transitional Sentence: _____
_____

Final Paragraph

Conclusion/Clincher: _____
_____
_____

Personal Thought: _____
_____
_____

Call to Action: _____
_____
_____

Contrast Essay

Introductory Paragraph

Topic Sentence: _____

_____

_____

Summarize the Details: _____

_____

_____

Why Does Reader Want to Know: _____

_____

_____

Detail Paragraph 1 (Subject One)   (first of all)

Topic Sentence: _____

_____

_____

Detail: _____

Elaborate: _____

_____

_____

Transitional Sentence: _____

_____

Contrast Essay

Detail Paragraph 2 (Subject Two)   (on the other hand)

Topic Sentence: _____

_____

_____

Detail: _____

Elaborate: _____

_____

_____

Transitional Sentence: _____

_____

Detail Paragraph 3 (Subject One)   (secondly)

Topic Sentence: _____

_____

_____

Detail: _____

Elaborate: _____

_____

_____

Transitional Sentence: _____

_____

Contrast Essay

Detail Paragraph 4 (Subject Two)   (however)

Topic Sentence: _____

_____

_____

Detail: _____

Elaborate: _____

_____

_____

Transitional Sentence: _____

_____

Detail Paragraph 5 (Subject One)   (last, finally)

Topic Sentence: _____

_____

_____

Detail: _____

Elaborate: _____

_____

_____

Transitional Sentence: _____

_____

Contrast Essay

Detail Paragraph 6 (Subject Two) (in contrast)

Topic Sentence: _____
_____
_____

Detail: _____

Elaborate: _____
_____
_____
_____

Transitional Sentence: _____
_____

Final Paragraph

Conclusion/Clincher: _____
_____
_____

Personal Thought: _____
_____
_____
_____

Call to Action: _____
_____
_____
_____

Transition Words

Also	Similarly	Likewise
In addition	First	Next
Then	Second	Third
Last	Finally	In conclusion
In summary	Therefore	Thus
To begin	Initially	In the beginning
For instance	For example	Again
As well	Meanwhile	In other words
However	Conversely	Although
As much as	On the other hand	Even though
Unfortunately	Sadly	Happily
Unexpectedly	Surprisingly	Furthermore
After that	In contrast	One way
Another way	Another reason	One reason

REFERENCE

DIAGRAM KEY

- S Subject
- V Verb
- O Object
- _ Adjective
- C Completer
- AV Adverb
- [ ] Phrase/Simile
- ▢ Subject Describer
- ✓ Interjection
- ◯ Parenthetical Expression
- △ Appositive

REFERENCE

Definitions

Adjective
A word that describes a person, place, or thing.

Adverb
A word that describes how, where, or when the action happened.

Appositive
A word or words that repeat the subject or object in a different way.
    EXAMPLE: Mt. Saint Helens, an active volcano, erupted in 1980.

Audience
The people you are writing for.

Chronological Sequencing
Sequencing events in the order that they occurred.

Comparative/Contrast Paragraph or Essay
A paragraph or essay that compares or contrasts how two things are similar or different.

Completer
A word used to complete an incomplete verb.

Compound Sentence
A sentence with two complete thoughts (subject and verb) that are joined with a connector (and/but) and a comma.

Conclusion
Final part of a paragraph or story that wraps up the paragraph with a logical ending.

Contraction
One word formed by combining and shortening two words.

Details
Parts of a paragraph that support the topic sentence.

Dialogue
The exact words that a character says.

Exclamation Point (!)
Punctuation at the end of a sentence that says something exciting.

Expository Writing
Writing that informs the reader.

First-Person Point of View
When the writer gives a straight forward account of the facts from his or her own perspective (uses I, me and my).

REFERENCE

General to Specific Sequencing
A method of sequencing that begins with a general statement and follows with reasons, specific examples, or facts to support the general statement.

How Phrase
A prepositional phrase that tells how the action occurred.

Informative Paragraph or Essay
A paragraph or essay that gives factual information about a particular subject.

Interjection
A word that interrupts a sentence to express a strong emotion or to indicate agreement or disagreement.

Memory Detail
Details from your own past experience.

Noun
A person, place, or thing.

Object
The person, place, or thing that receives the action.

Operational Paragraph or Essay
A paragraph or essay that explains a process.

Order of Importance Sequencing
Sequencing that either begins with the most important element and ends with the least important or begins with the least important element and ends with the most important.

Order of Location Sequencing
Sequencing that uses location words to help the reader picture the location of certain features.

Paragraph
Several sentences that together express an idea.

Parenthetical Expression
A word or phrase that adds a little more explanation to the words that follow.

    EXAMPLE: If it were up to me, I would choose the red one.

Period (.)
Punctuation at the end of a sentence that makes a statement.

Persuasive Paragraph or Essay
A paragraph or essay that attempts to persuade the reader to act or believe in a certain way.

Preposition
A word that shows the relationship between two nouns.

Pronoun
A small word substituted for a person, place, or thing ie; he, she.

REFERENCE

Proper Name
The actual name of a person, place, or thing ie; John.

Question Mark (?)
Punctuation at the end of a sentence that asks a question.

Quotation Marks (" ")
Punctuation that comes before the first word spoken and after the last word spoken in a dialogue.

Reflective Detail
Details you try to predict by imagining what would have been or what you hope might happen.

Run-On Sentence
Two or more complete thoughts joined without punctuation or connector words.

    EXAMPLE: Maria and her horse jumped over the gate they landed with grace.

Sensory Detail
Details you perceive through your senses (sight, smell, touch, hearing, and taste).

Sequencing
Putting information in a certain order.

Simile
A phrase that tells how the action occurred by using the words "like" or "as" to compare an object/person with the qualities of another object/person.

Story Elements:

    Topic Sentence — Tells the reader what the story will be about.

    Setting — Where and when the story takes place.

    Characters — People or animals in the story.

    Plot/Conflict — The main events in the story that surround a problem the character(s) must solve.

    Resolution — How the problem in the story is resolved.

    Lesson — What the character(s) learn by solving the problem.

Subject
The person, place, or thing that the sentence is about.

Subject Describer Phrases or Words
A phrase or word (other than an adjective) that tells which subject the sentence is about.

Third-Person Point of View
When the writer is coming from an observational or authoritative point of view (does not use I, me, and my).

REFERENCE

Topic Sentence
Usually the first sentence in a paragraph or story. It tells the reader what the paragraph or story is about.

When Phrase
A phrase that starts with a preposition and tells when the action took place.

Where Phrase
A phrase that starts with a preposition and tells where the action took place.

Why Phrase
A prepositional phrase that tells why the action occurred.

Verb
The action word in the sentence.

Adverbs

how	when	where
slowly	yesterday	north
quickly	today	south
sadly	tomorrow	east
happily	last night	west
loudly	this morning	left
quietly	tonight	right
madly	forever	straight
hastily	this afternoon	forward
wisely	tomorrow night	backward
knowingly	tomorrow morning	near
lovingly		far
casually		close
wildly		here
uncontrollably		there
easily		up
nervously		down
anxiously		
hesitantly		
softly		
lazily		
closely		
instantly		

REFERENCE

Prepositions

above	across	after	against
amid	among	around	at
along	before	behind	below
beneath	beyond	beside	between
by	during	down	for
from	in	inside	into
near	on	over	outside
out	off	of	onto
past	since	through	to
toward	under	until	up
underneath	upon	with	within
without			

Dialogue Words

saying	exclaimed	pondered
asked	stuttered	mumbled
thought	shouted	snapped
said	questioned	roared
announced	giggled	laughed
whispered	cackled	wondered
prayed	cried	